Traditional Indian Vegan and Vegetarian Cookbook

100 Easy Instant Pot Recipes for the Home.

Akshara Divya Gayathri

Traditional Indian Vegetarian Instant Pot Cookbook / Akshara Divya Gayathri-- 1st ed.
ISBN 9798519995580

I like to cook Indian food when I can. I find the process of creating a home-cooked meal to be unwinding.
—ARCHIE PANJABI

CONTENTS

CHAPTER ONE

INTRODUCTION

Instant Pot is known as a game-changer because it has come to revolutionize the world of cooking.

With the Instant Pot, cooking Indian food at home is not a difficult task anymore. It has demystified Indian cuisine for people worldwide.

Instant Pot has been a tremendous help for families who need a quick meal that is healthy and delicious without o can now have healthy and delicious meals without cooking in the kitchen for hours

For vegetarians and vegans, cooking this unique pressure cooker has been helpful to their overall diet. The beans cook evenly to your preference– without having to watch over it. And most diced potatoes cook in two minutes!

Even if you are not a vegetarian or vegan, you'll love this extensive collection of 100 Instant Pot recipes. So here's a running set of recipes that are Indian, Vegetarian and Vegan and made in an Instant Pot Pressure Cooker.

I am sure you'll find quite a few recipes that you and your family will enjoy!

with love,

Akshara Divya Gayathri

CHAPTER TWO

HOW TO CARE FOR YOUR INSTANT POT

All parts of the Instant Pot®, except for the cooker base, are dishwasher safe. This includes the stainless steel inner pot, the lid, the sealing ring, and the steam rack. The cooker base must be kept dry and wiped down with a damp cloth when necessary. The anti-block shield should be washed after each use and re-installed.

The inner Pot of the cooker (the stainless steel cooking pot), the sealing ring, the lid, and the steam rack are all dishwasher safe. Before cleaning, ensure the cooker is unplugged and has cooled down.

Cooker Base and Heating Element

The cooker base is home to the microprocessor and the heating element essential to cooking. Do Not Place in the Dishwasher! If the cooker base gets wet, allow it to dry completely.

Clean the exterior of the cooker base with a damp cloth. You can use a slightly wet cloth to clean the inside of the cooker. It is, however, important that the cooker be kept dry.

If you need to clean the area around the lip of the cooker, use a damp cloth or an old toothbrush to clean the edges.

Stainless Steel Inner Pot & Steam Rack

The inner Pot and the steam rack are made of sturdy, food-grade stainless steel (304 – 18/8) and are entirely dishwasher safe. For the most part, you can keep the inner Pot cleaned just as you would clean any stainless steel pot—by hand washing or the dishwasher.

Should the inner Pot develop harmless water stains, a non-abrasive scouring cleanser, made especially for cooking pots, brings back the original shine.

You can also periodically clean the inner Pot by placing 1 cup of white vinegar in the bottom of the inner Pot. Allow it to rest for 5 minutes, and then pour out the vinegar and rinse.

Removing Bluish Marks from Your Stainless Steel Inner Pot

Instant Pot's inner Pot (cooking pot) is stainless steel, food-grade 304 (18/8) with no chemical coating. It is durable and will retain its appearance for years to come with proper care.

It is not uncommon for a bluish or "rainbow" discoloration to appear on the inside of the Pot with stainless steel cookware. It may be easily removed by using a non-abrasive stainless steel cleaner, which will remove the marks and help retain the original brightness.

Another option is to cover the bottom with white vinegar. Allow the vinegar to sit for 5 minutes, remove, and rinse the inner Pot. The discoloration marks should be removed completely. For "White Hard Water" stains, they can be removed with a damp sponge soaked in vinegar or lemon.

Lid

The lid is top-rack dishwasher safe. It is best to remove the sealing ring and the anti-block shield so that the lid may be thoroughly cleaned. One way to prevent the lid from retaining odors is to place it upside down on the Pot until it has completely dried or you are ready to use it. Verify the steam release valve and float valve, and make sure there is no food or other debris that would block them, and prevent your cooker from coming to pressure

Anti-block Shield

The anti-block shield underneath the lid should be removed and cleaned after each use, especially following the preparation of foods that may splatter.

To remove, using your thumb, push the side of the anti-block shield towards the lid rim and lift up. It may take a little effort, but the anti-block shield should pop out.

You can now wash the shield with warm, soapy water. Rinse, wipe dry with a soft cloth, and place back in position when dry. To position the anti-block shield in place, push down.

Sealing Ring

The sealing ring is made of high-quality, heat-resistant silicone. It can be hand-washed with soapy water or placed in the dishwasher. Allow the ring to dry completely before inserting back into the lid. Ensure the sealing ring is positioned in the lid after every wash and that it is securely in place before you start cooking.

The sealing ring is critical in the functioning of your cooker. Scrutinize it after it is washed. Any sign of cracking or other damage, replace the sealing ring. Replace only with Genuine Instant Pot® sealing rings.

As silicone may pick up food odors during cooking, you may wish to have one sealing ring for savory and another for sweet foods.

Under normal conditions, it should be fine for 18 – 24 months. If you notice cracks, leaking, or deformation in the sealing ring, it should be replaced immediately. However, the sealing ring is porous and may absorb odors and become discolored. To avoid discoloration and odors, you may wish to change the sealing ring every 6 – 12 months.

Condensation Collector

The condensation collector is to be removed, and hand washed periodically. Allow drying before replacing.

CHAPTER THREE

COOKING TIPS

Before starting, ensure the inner Pot is positioned in the cooker base. If you have added water, ensure the exterior of the inner Pot is dry before positioning it in the cooker base.

Allow meats to "rest" 5-20 minutes (depending on the size of the cut) after cooking to ensure juiciness.

The cooker handles are also a lid holder. The lid has been designed with lid fins that fit perfectly inside the right- and left-handed cooker base handles.

Do not overfill the Instant Pot with food – it will cause the steam valve to clog.

Remember to turn off your Instant Pot. On older models, the 'Keep Warm/Cancel' buttons are the same, ensuring that when selected, the display indicates OFF.

Make sure the vent position is always at Sealing before you start Pressure Cooking, or else the steam will escape, and you'll end up with burnt food. Make sure the vent position is at Venting before you begin Slow Cooking.

Do not touch the lid's hot surfaces during or after cooking. Clean the steel insert and the lid after each use. DO NOT immerse the base unit in water.

Replace the silicone sealing ring every 18-24 months, as they will stretch over time with regular use.

Always ensure that the steam release handle/valve, steam release pipe, anti-block shield, float valve, and heating element are clean and free of food particles and debris before cooking.

DO NOT use the Quick release feature for sticky foods or foods like Porridge. This is because will food will start coming out of the steam valve and mess up your Instant Pot lid and possibly your countertop. This will also cause the steam valve/vent to block.

Cut larger pieces of food into smaller uniform sizes for even and thorough cooking.

To hasten pressurization when cooking large cuts of meat, allow the meat to "rest" at room temperature for 10-15 minutes before cooking.

All programs except Rice default to High Pressure. For Rice, the default is Low Pressure.

For the best rice results, leave the lid on after the cook cycle for an additional 5-10 minutes before quick releasing pressure.

When pressure cooking, always ensure the steam release handle/valve or quick-release button is in the "Sealing" position.

Pressure Cooking liquids must be water-based, such as stock, juice or broth.

Aloo Baingan Masala|Potato Eggplant Curry

This is a delicious and flavorful Punjabi dish made by cooking potatoes and eggplants with onions, tomatoes and few indian spices.

Servings: 4 Calories: 311kcal Course: curry, Main Course Prep Time: 10 mins Cook Time : 15 mins Total Time : 25 mins

Ingredients

3 medium potatoes
6-8 baby eggplant
1 medium onion finely chopped
2 medium tomato finely chopped
2 cloves garlic minced
1 inch ginger grated
1 tbs. oil
1 tsp. cumin (jeera) seeds
salt to taste
½ cup water
2 tbs. coriander leaves/cilantro finely chopped
A squeeze of fresh lemon juice

Dry Spices

½ tsp. turmeric powder
½ tsp. red chilli powder
1 tsp. coriander powder
½ tsp. garam masala

Directions

- Peel the potato skin and cut into 1 inch pieces. Also cut Eggplant(baingan) into large pieces, 1 to 1.5 inches
- Press SAUTE mode on Instant Pot. Add oil in to the POT.Once hot, add cumin seeds, let them splutter. Next add minced ginger, garlic and green chili. Saute for 30 secs.
- Add chopped onion and saute till onions turn light brown in color.

- Next add tomatoes, all the dry spices like turmeric powder, red chilli powder, coriander powder, garam masala and cook for 2 more mins till tomatoes turn soft.
- Then add potato, eggplant pieces, water, salt and mix well.Make sure to scrap of any spice if sticking to the pot.
- Close the lid on the pot, and turn valve from VENTING to SEALING position. Press CANCEL button on Instant Pot.
- Set the pot to MANUAL/PRESSURE COOK (High Pressure) and set timer to 3 MINS.When the instant pot beeps, Do a QUICK RELEASE by moving the valve from sealing to venting position.
- Remove lid away from you, squeeze in some lemon juice and garnish with cilantro (coriander leaves) and Mix well.
- Serve with hot with chapatis, roti & parathas.

Zucchini Curry | Courgette Curry

This is a creamy and delicious curry made with zucchini that are infused with spices.

Servings: 4 Calories: 138kcal Course: Main Course Prep Time: 10 mins Cook Time: 10 mins Total Time: 20 mins

Ingredients

2-3 medium zucchini
2 tablespoon olive oil
1 tsp. cumin (jeera) seeds
1 tbs. ginger and garlic minced
1 green chili finely chopped
1 medium onion finely chopped
2 medium tomatoes finely chopped or 1 can tomato sauce
¼ cup water
salt to taste
2 tbs. coconut cream or fresh cream, (optional but recommended)
1 tbs. lemon juice
2 tbs. cilantro/coriander leaves

Dry spices:

½ tsp. turmeric powder
½ tsp. red chilli powder
1 tsp. coriander powder
1 tsp. garam masala

Directions

- Wash and cut 2-3 zucchini lengthwise, and then into half-moon pieces (around 3-3.5 cups).
- Press SAUTE on Instant Pot. Add oil to the POT. Once hot, add cumin seeds, let them splutter.
- Then add minced ginger and garlic, green chili, Saute for 15 secs.
- Add chopped onions. Saute till it turns light brown in color.
- Next add tomatoes, dry spices like turmeric powder, red chili powder, coriander powder, garam masala powder, salt and cook for 2 more mins till the tomatoes turn soft.
- Then add all zucchini pieces, water, and mix well. Make sure to Deglaze the pot, scrape any spice that is sticking to the inner pot in order to avoid the BURN alert.
- Close the lid on the pot and turn pressure valve to SEALING position.
- Furthermore, Set the pot to MANUAL/PRESSURE COOK (High Pressure) and timer to 1 MINUTE. When the instant pot beeps, do a Quick Release (QR).
- Lastly, remove the lid away from you, add coconut cream or fresh cream and squeeze lemon juice, garnish with cilantro.
- Serve hot with chapatis, roti & parathas.

Vegetable and Paneer Biryani

This is a classic one pot meal full of flavors and aromas from whole spices, garam masala and the long grain basmati rice.

Servings: 6 Calories: 453kcal Course: Entrée Prep Time: 30 mins Cook Time: 20 mins Total Time: 50 mins

Ingredients

2 cups Extra long grain Basmati rice
2 cups water for soaking
3 tbs. ghee divided
1 large yellow onion thinly sliced
1 tsp. cumin seeds
4 whole green cardamoms
4 cloves
10 whole black peppercorns
2 bay leaves

1 cup carrots chopped lengthwise
1 cup green beans chopped into 1-inch pieces
1 cup white mushrooms halved
½ cup red pepper chopped into 1-inch pieces
½ cup corn
1 cup paneer cubed into ½ inch cubes
½ tbs. ginger grated
½ tbs. garlic minced
¼ tsp. ground turmeric
1 tsp. Kashmiri red chili powder
1 teaspoon garam masala
3 tsp.s kosher salt divided
2 cups water for cooking
2 tbs. fresh mint chopped
½ cup cilantro chopped

Directions

- Rinse and soak the rice in water for 20 mins. Drain water after 20 mins.
- Set the Instant Pot to SAUTE(More) mode and heat half of the ghee. Add sliced onions and cook for 5-7 mins or until the onions are lightly caramelized. Take half of the onions out and reserve for garnish.
- Add remaining ghee, cumin seeds, cardamom, cloves, black peppers, and bay leaves. Cook for 30 seconds. Add all the veggies (carrots, green beans, mushrooms, red pepper, corn, paneer). Press CANCEL and deglaze the pot removing any browning. Use 1 to 2 tbs. of water if needed.
- Add ginger, garlic, turmeric, red chili powder, garam masala, and half of the salt. mix well. Add mint, rice, and remaining salt. Add water. Mix well, making sure most of the rice is underwater.
- Close the Instant Pot with pressure valve to SEALING. Pressure Cook(low-pressure) for 5 mins followed by QUICK RELEASE. Open the Instant Pot. Garnish with caramelized onions and cilantro.
- Serve hot with Raita or yogurt.

Bombay Potatoes and Peas

Servings: 3 Calories: 232.3kcal Course: Main Prep Time: 15 mins Cook Time: 30 mins Total Time: 45 mins

Ingredients

2 tsp oil

1/2 tsp cumin seeds
1 tsp mustard seeds
1 small red onion chopped
1 large tomato
7 cloves of garlic
1 inch ginger chopped
1/2 tsp turmeric
1/2 tsp cayenne/ red chili powder or to taste
1 tsp ground coriander
1/2 tsp ground cumin
1/2 tsp homemade garam masala
3 medium potatoes chopped small
3/4 tsp or more salt
1 cup water
1 cup peas fresh or thawed if frozen
1/4 cup chopped cilantro

Directions

- Heat oil in a large skillet over medium heat. When the oil is hot, add cumin and mustard seeds. Cook until the cumin seeds change color.
- Add onions, mix and cook until translucent. 5 to 6 mins.
- Meanwhile, blend the tomato, garlic and ginger into a coarse puree.
- Add the tomato puree and spices to the pan. Cook until the puree thickens and garlic smells roasted. 5 to 6 mins.
- Add the potatoes, salt and water. Cover and cook for 10 to 11 mins.
- Add the peas, taste and adjust salt and spice. Reduce heat to medium-low. Simmer for another 10 to 12 mins or until the potatoes are cooked to preference. Add water if the potatoes start to stick or if you prefer more curry.
- Mix in the cilantro. Add some lemon juice if needed. Taste ad adjust salt and spice. Mix in. Serve hot.

Butternut Squash Lentil Curry
A hearty, healthy go-to comfort food for weeknight meals.

Serving size: 6 Prep Time: 15 mins Cook Time: 45 mins Total Time: 1 hr Course: Main course

Ingredients

1 1/2 tablespoons unrefined virgin coconut oil, divided

1 teaspoon whole cumin seeds
1 medium yellow onion, diced
1 1/2 teaspoons kosher salt, divided
6 garlic cloves, minced
1 piece of fresh ginger, finely minced or grated
1 tablespoon curry powder
1 1/2 teaspoons ground turmeric
1/2 teaspoon cayenne pepper (optional)
2 tablespoons water
5-6 cups peeled and roughly chopped butternut squash
1 1/2 cups low-sodium vegetable broth
1 cup brown lentils or green lentils
1 can coconut milk
3 tablespoons cashew butter
4 ounces baby kale or baby spinach
1 tablespoon fresh lemon or lime juice
1 large handful fresh cilantro, roughly chopped

Directions

- Rinse the lentils and drain them.
- Select the SAUTÉ setting on the Instant Pot and after a few minutes, add 1/2 tablespoon of the coconut oil, followed by the cumin seeds. Toss for 30-60 seconds until lightly browned and very fragrant.
- Add the remaining 1 tablespoon oil, followed by the onion and 1/2 teaspoon of the kosher salt. Cook the onion for 4-5 minutes until lightly browned. Then add the garlic and ginger and cook for 1 minute, stirring frequently to prevent sticking.
- Stir in the the curry powder, turmeric, and cayenne (if using) for 30 seconds, adding the 2 tbsp water to prevent the mixture from drying out too much.
- Add the chopped butternut squash and stir to coat it in the spice mixture. Pour in the vegetable broth and use a wooden spoon or spatula to scrape up any browned bits at the bottom of the pan.
- Then add the remaining 1 teaspoon kosher salt, the lentils, and coconut milk. Scoop the cashew butter on top but do not stir. This helps prevent the nut butter from sinking to the bottom and possibly triggering the Instant Pot burn warning.
- Secure the Instant Pot lid and set the Pressure Release to SEALING. Select the Pressure Cook or Manual setting and set the cook time for 10 minutes.
- Once the timer goes off, allow a NATURAL PRESSURE RELEASE. Once the pressure has released, open the pot and stir in the baby kale.

- Select the Sauté setting and heat for about 2 minutes or until the kale has wilted, then select Cancel. Add the lemon or lime juice and the cilantro and stir to combine.
- Serve the butternut squash lentil curry over white rice or with flatbread.

Beetroot Korma

This is a healthy curry made with beetroot cooked together in an aromatic spicy korma masala made of coconut, cashews and other spices.

Servings: 4 Calories: 232kcal Course: Main Course, Side Dish Prep Time: 10 mins Cook Time: 10 mins Total Time: 20 mins

Ingredients

2 cups beetroot chopped into small cubes
1 cup onion finely chopped
½ cup tomato finely chopped
1 tbs. ginger-garlic paste
½ tablespoon red chilli powder
1 tsp. coriander powder
½ tsp. jeera Powder (cumin powder)
1 tsp. garam masala powder
salt to taste
2 tbs. oil
1 tbs. coriander leaves/cilantro chopped for garnish
1 tablespoon lime juice
½ cup water or as required

For Grinding

¼ cup grated coconut fresh or frozen
6-8 cashew nuts
1 inch cinnamon
1 tsp. saunf (fennel seeds) optional
water for grinding

Directions

- Peel the beetroot and cut it into small cubes.
- Grind coconut, cashews, cinnamon to a smooth paste.
- Press SAUTE mode on Instant Pot. Add oil in to the POT.

- Once POT is hot add onions, ginger-garlic paste and saute until onions turn light brown.
- Next add chopped tomatoes and cook till they turn soft.
- Then add in the chopped beetroot, red chilli powder, garam masala powder, coriander powder, jeera powder, ground coconut-cashew paste, salt and mix well.
- Then add water and give a stir.
- Close the lid on the pot, and turn pressure valve to SEALING position.
- Set the pot to MANUAL/PRESSURE COOK (High Pressure) and set timer to 5 mins
- Do a NATURAL PRESSURE RELEASE (Wait until silver button on lid drops).
- Remove lid away from you, add lime juice and garnish with cilantro.Mix well.
- Serve with hot with pooris, chapatis, roti & parathas.

Chickpea Coconut Curry
This is a flavorful, healthy and easy to make for busy days.

Servings: 4 Calories: 380 Course: Main Course, Side Dish Prep Time : 10 mins Cook Time : 10 mins Total Time : 20 mins

Ingredients

1 tbs. coconut oil
1 bay leaf (optional)
1 tsp. cumin (jeera) seeds
1 medium onion finely chopped
1 tbs. ginger garlic minced
1 cup crushed tomatoes or tomato puree
1 can (15 oz each) chickpeas
1 can (13.5 oz) coconut milk
salt to taste
1 tbs. lemon juice
2-3 cups baby spinach

Dry Spices:

¼ tsp. turmeric powder
½ tsp. red chilli powder
1 tsp. garam masala powder
1 tsp. coriander powder

Directions

- Press SAUTE mode on Instant Pot. Add oil in to the POT.Once oil is hot add cumin seeds, bay leaf and let cumins splutter.
- Then add onions, ginger garlic paste and saute until onions turn light brown for 3-4 mins.
- Next add the crushed tomatoes along with the juice or tomato puree and the spices like red chilli powder, turmeric powder, garam masala powder, coriander powder and cook for 2 mins.Make sure to Deglaze the bottom of the pot to remove any stuck bits.
- Lastly add canned or cooked chickpeas, coconut milk and salt. Stir well. If you think mixture is too thick add ½ cup of water to this.
- Close the lid on the pot, and turn pressure valve to SEALING position.
- Set the pot to MANUAL/PRESSURE COOK (High Pressure) and set timer to 3 mins. Once the pot beeps, do a 5-minute NATURAL PRESSURE RELEASE(NPR) and then release the remaining pressure manually.
- While the curry is still warm, add in the spinach and fresh lemon juice and mix until spinach has fully wilted. Dont worry if the curry is too liquid consistency. Just turn on SAUTE mode again and boil the curry for 2-3 mins or until you get desired consistency.
- Serve with hot with Basmati rice or quinoa.

Curried Potato Cauliflower

Servings: 4 Calories: 107kcal Course: Main course Prep Time: 10 mins Cook Time: 20 mins Total Time: 30 mins

Ingredients

1/2 small onion
2 tomatoes
6 to 7 cloves of garlic
1 inch ginger
1/2 hot green chile
1 tsp oil
1/2 tsp turmeric
1 tsp ground cumin
1/2 to 1 tsp garam masala
3/4 to 1 tsp salt
1/2 tsp paprika
2 medium potatoes cubed
1 small cauliflower chopped into large florets

cayenne/pepper flakes, garam masala, cilantro and lemon for garnish

Directions

- Blend the onion, tomato, garlic, ginger, green chile until smooth.
- Put the Instant Pot on SAUTE mode. When hot, add oil. (* At this point you can add 1/2 tsp cumin seeds and cook until they darken slightly.) Add the onion tomato puree to the pot. Rinse the blender using 1-2 tbsp of water and add to the pot.
- Add the spices and potato and mix well. Cover with a glass lid that fits the pot and cook for 4-5 mins.
- Add the cauliflower and mix in well. Close the Pot lid to SEALING. Select MANUAL 2 mins for LOW PRESSURE(preferred) Or 0 mins on HIGH PRESSURE.
- RELEASE PRESSURE with QUICK RELEASE carefully. Add cayenne, a sprinkle of garam masala, cilantro and lemon juice to taste.
- Serve hot with Dals or Curries and flatbread or rice.

Brown Rice Mung Bean Kitchari | Mung Bean Stew
Servings: 4 Calories: 209kcal Course: Main Prep Time: 20 mins Cook Time: 20 mins Total Time: 40 mins

Ingredients

1/2 cup mung beans dry
1/2 cup brown basmati rice
1/2 tsp oil
1/2 tsp cumin seeds
1/2 cup chopped red onion
2 medium tomatoes
5 cloves garlic
1 inch ginger
1/2 tsp turmeric
1 tsp ground coriander
1/2 tsp garam masala
1/4 to 1/2 tsp cayenne
1/4 tsp black pepper
3.5 - 4 cups water 1/2 cup less for thicker
1 tsp lemon juice
3/4 to 1 1/4 tsp salt

Directions

- Soak the beans and rice for atleast 15 mins. Soak at this step as the next few steps take 15 to 20 mins
- Blend the onions, tomato, garlic, ginger, spices with a few tbsp of water to a smooth puree and keep aside.
- Start the Instant Pot (IP) on SAUTE at normal heat.
- When hot, add oil, let the oil heat up for a few seconds, then add cumin seeds. Roast the seeds for half a minute or until fragrant.
- Add the puree carefully, stir and cook until the puree thickens and smells roasted. 15 to 17 mins. Switch the SAUTE to off.
- Drain the beans and rice and add to the IP. Add water, salt, lemon juice. Mix. Add chopped veggies if you like.
- Close the lid. Press MANUAL and adjust time for 10 mins.
- Brown Basmati Rice soaked for 15 mins will cook in the 10 minute time. You might need to cook longer depending on the rice used (15 to 20 mins).
- The IP will start heating, and show "On" and then count down the mins when the pressure has reached.
- Once done, let the PRESSURE RELEASE NATURALLY. Or if you are are in a hurry. Try the QUICK RELEASE after 5 to 7 mins. If the rice or beans are not cooked to preference, you can cook them on SAUTE until they are tender.
- Taste and adjust salt and spice. Serve hot with crackers or toasted bread.

Lemon Rice

Servings:4 Calories: 175 kcal Course: Main course Prep Time: 30 mins Cook Time: 8 mins Total Time: 38 mins

Ingredients

1 cup basmati rice
3 tbs. oil of choice
1 tsp. black mustard seeds
1 tbs. split chickpeas (chana dal)
1 tbs. split and skinless black lentils (urad dal)
⅓ cup raw peanuts
15 curry leaves
1 Serrano pepper or green chili, adjust to taste
1 tsp. minced ginger
1 tsp. coriander powder
1 tsp. salt
½ tsp. turmeric

¼ cup lemon juice
2 tsp.s lemon zest optional
1 cup water

Directions

- Soak the basmati rice in cold water for 15-30 mins. Drain the water, rinse and set aside.
- Press the SAUTE´ button, add the oil and allow it to heat up for a minute. Add the mustard seeds, split chickpeas, split/skinless black lentils. After 1-2 mins, or once the lentils turn golden in color, add the raw peanuts and stir-fry.
- Add the curry leaves, Serrano pepper, ginger, coriander powder, salt and turmeric. Stir-fry for 30 seconds, then add lemon juice, lemon zest, water and rice. Mix well.
- Secure the lid, close the pressure valve and cook for 6 mins at high pressure.
- NATURALLY RELEASE PRESSURE for 10 mins. Open the valve to release any remaining pressure.
- Fluff the rice with a fork and serve.

Langarwali Dal

Servings: 4 Calories: 269kcal Course: Main Course Prep Time: 10 Mins Cook Time: 45 Total Time: 1 Hour 15 Mins

Ingredients

½ cup whole urad dal
¼ cup chana dal (split chickpeas)
3 tbs. ghee
1 tsp. cumin seeds
1 cup finely chopped onion
1 tbs. minced ginger
2 garlic cloves, minced
2 serrano chilies, seeded and finely chopped
1 cup chopped Roma tomatoes
1 tsp. salt
½ tsp. turmeric powder
1 tsp. Kashmiri chili powder
1 tsp. garam masala
2 tsp. coriander powder
1 tsp. cumin powder
¼ cup chopped cilantro plus 3 tbs. for garnishing

2 cups water
1-2 tsp. unsalted butter

Directions

- Wash and soak urad and chana dal in warm water while you prepare other ingredients and start sautéing the onions.
- Preheat the instant pot by selecting SAUTÉ. When the inner pot is hot, after about 30 seconds, add the ghee and cumin seeds.
- When the cumin seeds begin to sizzle, add the onion, ginger, garlic, and serrano chilies, then stir and cook for 2 mins.
- Add the tomatoes, salt, turmeric, Kashmiri chili powder, garam masala, coriander, and cumin powder. Stir and cook for 3 mins, until the tomatoes break down.
- Rinse and drain the soaked lentils and add them to the pot. Add the cilantro and water. Stir, scraping off any brown bits stuck to the bottom. Turn off sauté.
- Lock the lid in place. Select manual or pressure cook and adjust to high. Cook for 40 mins on SEALING mode.
- When the cooking is complete, wait 10 mins for NATURAL PRESSURE RELEASE, after which follow the quick-release method as per your cooker Directions. Unlock and remove the lid.
- Stir the lentils and mash a few beans using a potato masher. This gives a creamy texture and thickens the curry. Stir in the butter (if using) to enhance creaminess.
- Garnish with the reserved cilantro and serve with Roti or cumin rice.

Baingan Bharta Recipe | Spiced Mashed Eggplant

Servings: 4 Calories: 55kcal Course: Main Prep Time: 5 mins Cook Time: 20 mins Total Time: 25 mins

Ingredients

2 tsp oil
1/2 tsp cumin seeds
3/4 cup onion (chopped)
1 inch ginger (finely chopped)
5 cloves of garlic (finely chopped)
1 hot green chilli (such as serrano - finely chopped)
1 tsp turmeric
1/2 tsp garam masala

1 tsp ground coriander
1/2 tsp smoked paprika
1 large tomato (diced)
1 large eggplant (peeled and cubed into small about half an inch cubes)
3/4 tsp salt
1/2 cup water
1/3 cup peas
1/4 cup cilantro

Directions

- Set your instant pot to SAUTÉ, once it has heated up, add oil. Let the oil heat up and add the cumin seeds. Cook for half a minute. Add the onion, ginger, garlic, green chili and a good pinch of salt. Cook for 3 minutes.
- Add all the ground spices and mix well. Then add the tomato and allow to cook for 2 minutes. Mash the larger pieces of tomato and deglaze with a tbsp of water if needed.
- Once the tomato is tender, add the eggplant, salt, water and give it a good mix. Cancel sauté mode, close the lid, then pressure cook for 9-10 minutes. Let the PRESSURE RELEASE NATURALLY.
- Open the lid and mash the eggplants really well using a potato masher. Taste and adjust the salt and flavor as needed. Add 1/2 teaspoon of liquid smoke for additional smoky flavor. Press sauté mode and cook for 3 minutes, stirring occasionally, (cook a few mins longer for thicker and more roasted) then add the peas and cilantro and mix in. Cancel sauté.
- Serve hot and garnish with additional cilantro, pepper flakes and sprinkle smoked paprika.

Spiced Yellow Lentils

Servings: 2 Calories: 192 kcal Course: Main course Prep Time: 10 mins Cook Time: 30 mins Total Time: 40 mins

Ingredients

1 cup split pigeon peas (toor dal)
1 tbs. oil
1 tsp. cumin seeds
1 serrano slit in half
½ cup frozen or fresh/thawed onion masala
1 tsp. salt
¼ tsp. garam masala

3 cups water
Cilantro to garnish

Directions

- Soak the lentils in cold water for 15-20 mins. Drain, rinse and set aside.
- Press the SAUTÉ button, add the oil and allow it to heat up for a minute. Add the cumin seeds and serrano pepper to the pot. Once the cumin seeds brown, add the remaining ingredients to the pot.
- Secure the lid, close the pressure valve and cook for 7 mins at high pressure.
- NATURALLY RELEASE PRESSURE (or wait 15 mins, then release remaining pressure)
- Garnish with cilantro and serve.

Onion Tomato Masala

This onion masala is the base for a number of Indian recipes! Make it in bulk and freeze for quick meals on busy days!

Servings: 3 Cups Calories: 255 Kcal Course: Sauce Prep Time: 20 Mins Cook Time: 50 Mins Total Time:1 Hr 10 Mins

Ingredients

4 tablespoons oil, use oil of choice
4 medium yellow onion, diced
10 large garlic cloves, chopped
2 inch ginger 22 grams, chopped
2 green chilies chopped
5 medium tomatoes, chopped
2 teaspoons coriander powder
1 teaspoon cumin powder
1/2 teaspoon garam masala
1/4 teaspoon red chili powder or adjust to taste
1/4 teaspoon turmeric
1 teaspoon salt
1-2 tablespoons water

Directions

- Press the SAUTE button on your Instant Pot, then press the adjust button to set saute to "more". Once it displays hot, add the oil to the pot and then add the diced onion.
- Saute the onions, stirring often. After around 13 minutes, the onions will turn nice golden brown in color. You want the onions to reach this color.
- Then add the garlic, ginger and green chilies and cook for 2 minutes.
- Add the chopped tomatoes, stir and cook for 2 more minutes.
- Then add the spices - coriander powder, cumin powder, garam masala, red chili powder and turmeric. Also add salt and mix everything.
- Add 1-2 tablespoons water to de-glaze the pot, scraping the bottom, there shouldn't be any burnt bits.
- Close the pot with its lid and press the manual or pressure cook button. Cook on high pressure for 10 minutes. Let the PRESSURE RELEASE NATURALLY.
- Open the pot once the pin comes down. If the masala looks too watery, press the saute button again and then then use the adjust button to set saute to "more". Saute (on more) for 3 to 4 minutes to get rid of excess water.
- Unplug the Instant pot and let the masala cool down a bit and transfer to a blender. Grind the masala to a smooth paste using your blender.
- Let the onion tomato masala cool completely and then freeze in individual portions.
- Use the masala as needed for your curries, sabzis, dal, stews etc. You may thaw the masala before using.

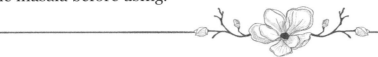

Veggie Lentil Dhansak

Servings: 2 Calories: 274kcal Course: Main Prep Time: 15 mins Cook Time: 30 mins Total Time: 45 mins

Ingredients

Dal and Veggies:

3/4 cup total split dals combination of red lentils and yellow lentils
2 cups chopped vegetables
1 cup packed chopped greens such as spinach, or fresh fenugreek leaves
1 tbsp minced ginger
4 cloves of garlic minced
1 hot green chile minced
1/2 tsp turmeric
3/4 tsp salt
1/2 tsp garam masala, coriander powder and a good pinch of ground cloves

Tempering:

1 tsp oil
3/4 tsp mustard seeds
1/2 tsp cumin seeds
1/2 cup chopped onion
3 cloves of garlic finely chopped
1/2 tsp salt

Directions

- Soak the dals for 15 mins to half hour. Drain and combine in Instant pot with the vegetables, and the rest of the ingredients under Dals and Veggies with 2.5 to 3 cups water.
- Cook for 3 mins on MANUAL (HIGH PRESSURE). Let the PRESSURE RELEASE NATURALLY.
- Meanwhile, make the tempering. Heat oil in a small skillet over medium heat. When the oil is hot, add mustard and cumin seeds and let them start to pop.
- Add onion and garlic and cook until golden, stirring occasionally. (a heavy bottom pan, a pinch of salt and stirring at regular intervals gives an even golden onion)
- Once the pressure has released, open the lid. At this point you can mash the veggies and lentils for a more traditional version.
- Mix in half the tempering into the lentil vegetable mixture in the Instant Pot.
- Taste and adjust salt and heat(cayenne). Add more salt and garam masala if needed. Garnish with the remaining half tempering, cilantro and lemon juice and serve.
- Serve with rice, flatbread, toasted bread or garlic bread

Easy Indian Potatoes / Aloo ki sabji / Batata Bhaji
This classic Indian Potato recipe is this easy and quick side dish.

Servings: 6 Calories: 187kcal Course: Side Dish Prep Time: 10 Mins Cook Time: 10 Mins Total Time: 20 Mins

Ingredients

2 tbs. peanut oil or olive oil
½ tsp. mustard seeds
½ tsp. cumin seeds (jeera)
⅛ tsp. asafoetida (hing)

6 curry leaves (kadipatta)
1 cup chopped onions
2 green chilies finely chopped
1-inch piece ginger grated
4 garlic cloves minced
½ tsp. turmeric powder
1 tsp. salt
6 medium-sized potatoes, peeled and chopped 4 cups chopped
1 tbs. squeezed lime juice
1 cup water

For garnishing

2 tbs. chopped cilantro

Directions

- Set the Instant Pot to 'SAUTE' mode and adjust the setting to 'More'. When the display reads 'Hot', add oil. When the oil heats up, add mustard seeds, cumin seeds (jeera) and hing (if using).
- When the mustard and cumin seeds start to sputter, add curry leaves and onions along with turmeric powder. Fry them till the onions have softened up and turned transparent (takes about 5 mins).
- Add green chilies, minced garlic, grated ginger, and salt. Mix well and saute it for about 30 seconds.
- Add potatoes along with ¾ cup water. Mix well and scrape the pot to remove any food particles stuck to the bottom.
- Close the vent and set it to the SEALING position. Pressure cook on high for 5 mins.
- Once the cooking cycle is complete, immediately release pressure by moving the vent to the venting position.
- The potatoes will be slightly smushed and that is okay. If you prefer dry, you can saute it for a minute or two on high heat to reduce the moisture.
- Open the lid and add lime juice. Mix well to combine.
- Garnish with chopped cilantro, if desired and Serve hot with rice and dal or ghee laden rotis.

Sookha Kala Chana | Spiced Brown Chickpeas

Servings: 8 Calories: 222 kcal Course: Main course Prep Time: 5 mins Cook Time: 45 mins Total Time: 50 mins

Ingredients

2 cups dried brown chickpeas (kala chana)
2 tbs. oil of choice
½ tsp. cumin seeds
½ tsp. black mustard seeds

Spices

1 black cardamom
½ tsp. coriander powder
½ tsp. dried mango powder amchur
½ tsp. garam masala
½ tsp. turmeric
¼ tsp. black pepper
¼ tsp. black salt
¼ tsp. paprika
¼ tsp. roasted cumin powder
⅛ - ¼ tsp. cayenne (optional)
1 tsp. salt
1 cup water
Cilantro to garnish

Directions

- Soak the brown chickpeas in cold water overnight. Drain, rinse and set aside.
- Press the SAUTE´ button, add the oil and allow it to heat up for a minute. Add the cumin seeds and mustard seeds. Once the cumin seeds become brown and the mustard seeds begin to pop, add the brown chickpeas and all of the spices. Mix well, then add the water.
- Secure the lid, close the pressure valve and cook for 30 mins at high pressure.
- NATURALLY RELEASE PRESSURE.
- Press the SAUTE´ button to boil o any remaining water in the pot.
- Garnish with cilantro.

Coconut Rice

Perfectly cooked rice with the sweet aroma and flavor of coconut milk. A great rice side dish to many Indian dishes!

Servings: 4 Calories: 280 kcal Course: Side Dish Prep Time: 2 mins Cook Time: 28 mins Total Time: 30 mins

Ingredients

1 cup Jasmine rice or Basmati rice rinsed
1 cup Coconut Milk unsweetened
¼ cup Water or Unsalted stock
¼ tsp Salt

Garnish Options:

Black Sesame Seeds
Spring Onions
Toasted Coconut flakes

Directions

- Add the rice, coconut milk, water and salt to the instant pot steel insert.
- Set the instant pot to the "Rice" function. This will default to 12 mins at low pressure. (4 mins at high pressure will work too)
- When the cooking time is done, let the PRESSURE RELEASE NATURALLY for 10 mins, then release the pressure manually.
- Add garnish of your choice and serve warm.

Vegetable Masala Pasta

Servings: 4 Calories: 357 kcal Course: Main course Prep Time: 10 mins Cook Time: 5 mins Total Time: 15 mins

Ingredients

2 ½ cups diced veggies (bell pepper, carrots, red onion, frozen corn, frozen peas)
2 cups elbow macaroni
1 ½ cups water
1 cup fresh or thawed onion masala
2 tbs. ghee/butter or oil
½ tsp. salt
½ tsp. garam masala

¼ tsp. cayenne adjust to taste
Cilantro to garnish (optional)

Directions

- Add all of the ingredients to the pot and mix well.
- Secure the lid, close the pressure valve and cook for 4 mins at high pressure.
- QUICK RELEASE PRESSURE as soon as it's done to avoid overcooking the pasta. Then quickly give the pasta a stir and transfer the contents of the pot to another bowl to stop the cooking process.
- Garnish with cilantro and serve.

Saag

Servings: 4 Calories: 327 kcal Course: Main course Prep Time: 5 mins Cook Time: 20 mins Total Time: 25 mins

Ingredients

2 tbs. ghee
2 onions diced
4 tsp. minced garlic
2 tsp. minced ginger

Spices

2 tsp. salt to taste
1 tsp. coriander
1 tsp. ground cumin
1 tsp. garam masala
½ tsp. black pepper
½ tsp. cayenne adjust to taste
½ tsp. turmeric
1 pound spinach rinsed
1 pound mustard leaves rinsed
dried fenugreek leaves
Ghee or butter

Directions

- Press the "SAUTE" button on the Instant Pot and add the ghee. Once it melts, add the onion, garlic, ginger and spices to the pot and stir-fry for 2-3 mins.

- Add the spinach, stirring until it wilts and there's enough room to add the mustard greens.
- Secure the lid, close the pressure valve and cook for 15 mins at high pressure.
- NATURALLY RELEASE PRESSURE.
- Remove the lid and use an immersion blender to puree the contents of the pot.
- Stir in the dried fenugreek leaves.
- Serve with ghee.

Jackfruit Curry

An easy to make curry made with warm indian spices and bursting with flavor!

Serving size: 4 Course: Dinner Prep Time: 30 mins Cook Time: 45 mins Total Time: 1 hr 15 mins

Ingredients

1 tablespoon refined coconut oil
1 1/2 teaspoons cumin seeds
1 1/2 teaspoons black mustard seeds
1 large yellow onion, diced
6 cloves garlic, minced
2- inch piece fresh ginger, minced or grated
1 serrano pepper, diced
1 teaspoon ground turmeric
2 teaspoons garam masala
1 teaspoon coriander
1 teaspoon sweet or hot paprika
1 teaspoon Indian red chili pepper
4-6 curry leaves
1 1/2 teaspoons kosher salt
3/4 cup water
1 can full-fat coconut milk
2 (20-ounce cans jackfruit) (in water or brine), drained and rinsed and pulled apart with fingers
3 medium sweet potatoes, peeled and diced into 3/4-inch cubes
1 8-ounce can tomato sauce
4-5 cups baby spinach or baby kale, roughly chopped
1 tablespoon freshly squeezed lemon juice
1/2 cup fresh cilantro chopped

Directions

- Select the SAUTÉ setting on the Instant Pot. After a few minutes, add the oil to heat up. Once the Instant Pot displays reads "HOT," add the cumin seeds and mustard seeds and fry for 45 seconds.
- Add the onions and cook until softened, about 5-6 minutes.
- Add the garlic, ginger, and pepper, and cook for 90 seconds, stirring frequently to prevent burning.
- Add the ground spices (turmeric, garam masala, coriander, paprika, and chili powder), curry leaves, and the 1 1/2 teaspoons kosher salt.
- Stir to coat and cook for 30 seconds, stirring to combine. Add the 3/4 water to deglaze, using a wooden spoon to scrape up any browned bits on the bottom of the pot.
- Pour in the coconut milk, followed by the shredded jackfruit and chopped sweet potatoes. Stir to combine and select Cancel.
- Secure the lid and set the Pressure Release to Sealing. SELECT the Pressure Cook setting at high pressure and set the cook time to 6 minutes.
- Once the timer has completed, allow a NATURAL PRESSURE RELEASE for 10 minutes and then switch the Pressure Release knob from Sealing to Venting to release any remaining steam.
- Open the pot and add the tomato sauce and spinach, and stir to incorporate. Select the SAUTÉ setting, bring the curry to a boil, and simmer until the sauce has thickened, about 2-3 minutes. Stir in the lemon juice and cilantro.
- Serve with white basmati rice or flatbread.

Chana Masala Recipe

A healthy protein recipe cooked in a spicy, flavorful onion-tomato gravy along with few spices.

Servings: 4 Calories: 281kcal Course: Side Dish Prep Time: 10 mins Cook Time : 25 mins Total Time : 35 mins

Ingredients

1 cup dry chickpeas soaked overnight
2 tbs. oil
1 tsp. cumin (jeera) seeds
1 bay leaf (tej patta)
1 medium onion finely chopped
1 tablespoon ginger-garlic paste
1 green chilli finely chopped

2 large tomato made into tomato puree
1 tsp. amchur powder (dry mango powder) or juice of half lemon
2 tbs. cilantro/coriander leaves
1 tbs. dried kasuri methi (optional)
1.5 cups water
salt to taste

Spices:

1 tsp. coriander powder
1 tablespoon chana (chole masala)
1 tsp. red chilli powder
¼ tsp. turmeric powder

Directions

- Soak Chickpeas for at least 4+ hours or overnight. Drain water and keep aside.
- Press SAUTE mode on Instant Pot. Add oil in to the POT.Once oil is hot add cumin seeds, bay leaf and let cumins splutter.
- Then add onions, green chillies, ginger garlic paste and saute until onions turn light brown for 3-4 mins.
- Next add tomato puree and the spices like red chilli powder, turmeric powder, chole masala powder, coriander powder and cook for 2 mins.
- Lastly add soaked chickpeas, salt and water. Stir well.
- Close the lid on the pot, and turn pressure valve to SEALING position.
- Set the pot to MANUAL/PRESSURE COOK (High Pressure) and set timer to 30 mins.
- Once the pot beeps, do a NATURAL PRESSURE RELEASE.
- Remove lid away from you, add amchur powder, kasuri methi and garnish with cilantro.Mix well.
- Dont worry if the curry is too liquid consistency. Just turn on SAUTE mode again and boil the curry for 5 mins or until you get desired consistency.
- Serve with hot with Bathura, pooris, chapatis, roti & parathas.

Aloo Beans|Potato & Green Beans

This is a popular north Indian dry curry made with potatoes, green beans and few spices.

Servings: 3 Calories: 204kcal Course: Main Course, Side Dish Prep Time : 10 mins
Cook Time : 10 mins Total Time : 20 mins

Ingredients

1 tablespoon oil
½ tsp. cumin seeds (jeera)
1 green chili finely chopped
1 small onion finely chopped
1 tsp. ginger minced
2 cups french beans cut into ½ inch
1 medium potato diced thinly into 1-inch length
salt to taste
¼ cup water
1 tbs. lemon juice or ½ tsp of amchur powder

Spices

½ tsp. red chilli powder adjust to taste
1 tsp. coriander powder
½ tsp. turmeric powder (haldi)
½ tsp. garam masala

Directions

- Press SAUTE mode on Instant Pot. Add oil in to the POT.Once hot, add cumin seeds, let them splutter.
- Next add minced ginger, green chili, onions and Stir-fry onions for 2-3 mins, or until it begins to brown.
- Add the chopped green beans, potatoes, water, coriander powder, turmeric ,red chilli powder ,salt and mix well.Make sure to scrap of any spice if sticking to the pot.
- Close the lid on the pot, and turn pressure valve to SEALING position.
- Set the pot to MANUAL/PRESSURE COOK (High Pressure) and set timer to 2 mins.
- When the instant pot beeps, Do a QUICK RELEASE.
- Remove lid away from you, sprinkle garam masala and lemon juice, Mix well. If there is any water, change the setting to saute mode and get it to your desired consistency.
- Serve with hot with chapatis, roti & parathas.

Kerala Kadala Curry| Brown Chickpeas in Coconut Curry

This is a popular accompaniment usually served with Appam or Puttu.

Servings: 4 Calories: 225 Course: Main Course, Side Dish Prep Time: 6 hours Cook Time: 30 mins Total Time: 6 hours 30 mins

Ingredients

For Masala Paste:

2 medium tomatoes
3 garlic cloves
1 inch ginger
2 cloves
1 cardamom
1 tsp. fennel seeds (saunf)

Other Ingredients:

1 cup kala chana/kadala/brown chickpeas
1 medium onion finely chopped
½ tsp. turmeric powder
1 tsp. red chilli powder
1 tsp. coriander powder
1 tsp. garam masala powder
1 tablespoon coconut oil
2 cups water
salt to taste

For Coconut Paste:

½ cup shredded coconut (fresh or frozen) or full fat coconut milk
½ cup water

For Tempering:

2 tsp.s coconut oil
½ tsp. mustard seeds
¼ tsp. cumin (jeera) seeds
a big pinch asafetida (hing)
1 stalk curry leaves
2 dry red chillies

Directions

- Soak chana (black chickpeas) overnight or for atleast 6 hours.
- Grind the tomatoes, ginger, garlic, cloves, cardamom and fennel seeds to a smooth paste. No need to add any water while grinding. Keep aside.
- Also grind the fresh coconut with half cup of water to a fine paste. Keep aside.
- **Note: You can also roast the coconut and then grind. If you dont have fresh coconut, you can also use ½ cup of full fat coconut milk instead.
- Press SAUTE mode on Instant Pot. Add oil in to the POT.Once POT is hot add onions and saute until onions turn light brown for 3-4 mins.
- Next add the masala paste and cook for 2-3 mins.
- Add the soaked chickpeas, spices like turmeric powder, red chilli powder, coriander powder, garam masala, salt and water for cooking. Stir well.
- Close the lid on the pot. Set the pot to "BEAN/CHILI" Mode and set timer to 30 mins.
- Do a NATURAL PRESSURE RELEASE.
- Meanwhile prepare the tempering. Heat 2 tsp. of oil, add mustard seeds, cumin seeds, curry leaves, dry red chillies, asafetida (hing) and sauté for 30 seconds and keep aside.
- Once the pressure has released naturally add the ground coconut paste and press sauté to cook for 3-4 mins. Adjust the consistency by adding water if required. Finally, add the tempering to the curry.
- Serve curry with appam or puttu.

Easy Lentil Brown Rice Soup

Servings: 4 Calories: 205kcal Course: Soup Prep Time: 15 mins Cook Time: 50 mins Total Time: 1 hr 5 mins

Ingredients

1/2 cup brown lentils
1/3 cup brown rice uncooked rice
1 tsp oil
1/2 tsp cumin seeds
1/2 tsp mustard seeds optional
1 bay leaf
1/2 medium onion chopped
4 cloves garlic finely chopped
1 inch ginger finely chopped
1 green chile chopped
1/2 tsp turmeric

1/2 tsp paprika
1/2 tsp garam masala or curry powder
1 tsp coriander powder
1/4 tsp chipotle pepper
1/4 tsp black pepper
1.5 cups diced tomatoes
2 tsp ketchup optional
1 tsp lemon juice
2 cups of veggies
3.5 cups water
3/4 tsp salt
1 cup chopped or baby spinach
lemon juice garam masala and cayenne for garnish

Directions

- Wash and Soak the lentil and rice for atleast 15 mins before using.
- Heat oil in IP and SAUTE, add cumin seeds, mustard seeds and cook until fragrant or they change color.
- Add bay leaf, onion, garlic ginger, chile and cook until translucent. about 5 mins. Add the spices and mix in. Roast for half a minute
- Add the tomatoes and splash of water and cook until the tomatoes are saucy. mash the larger pieces. Add lemon juice, ketchup, veggies, salt and mix in.
- Drain and add lentils, rice, water/broth and mix in.
- Cover and cook on Manual 18-20 mins with NATURAL RELEASE.
- Fold in the spinach in the last 5 mins.
- Add a sprinkle garam masala, cayenne to taste and more lemon if needed.
- Serve with crackers or papaddum.

One pot Moong dal khichdi | Lentil Porridge
This one-pot, comfort meal is easy on your stomach and is perfect for all ages.

Servings: 4 Calories: 297kcal Course: Main Course Prep Time: 2 Mins cook Time: 10 Mins total Time: 12 Mins

Ingredients

1 tablespoon ghee
1 tsp. jeera cumin seeds
¾ cup moong dal
¾ cup rice

salt to taste
½ tsp. turmeric powder
a pinch of hing asafoetida (optional)
4 cups of water

Directions

- Add oil in the steel insert of the Instant Pot and press the SAUTE function. Press the Adjust button to move the selection to "low" and wait till the display reads "Hot." Add cumin seeds and when they start to splutter, add the rinsed rice, moong dal along with salt, turmeric powder, and asafoetida. Add about 4 cups of water and mix well.
- Press "Warm / Cancel" button and then select "Pressure Cook." Adjust the time to 10 mins and pressure selection to high or alternatively select the "Porridge" setting. Cover the Instant Pot lid and lock it. Make sure the vent is at SEALING position.
- Wait until the vent returns to the venting position before checking on the khichdi.
- Serve hot with a side of curd and pickle.

Beans Poriyal | Green Beans with Coconut

Servings: 4 Calories: 117kcal Course: Main Course Prep Time: 5 Mins Cook Time: 10 Mins Total Time: 15 Mins

Ingredients

4 cups finely chopped green beans
2 tbs. coconut oil
¼ tsp. mustard seeds
1 sprig of curry leaves
2 green chilies slit lengthwise
¼ cup finely cut onions (optional)
2 garlic cloves crushed
¼ tsp. turmeric powder (optional)
salt to taste
2 tbs. freshly grated coconut (optional)

Directions

- If you are using fresh beans then rinse and drain them after chopping. Set it aside.

- Add oil to the steel insert of the Instant Pot and press the SAUTE function. Press the ADJUST button to move the selection to "Normal" and wait till the display reads "Hot."
- Add mustard seeds and when they start spluttering, add curry and green chilies. Let it fry for around 20 seconds and then add chopped onions along with garlic. Fry them till they have softened (approximately 5-6 mins).
- Add chopped beans, turmeric powder (if using), and salt. Give it a stir. If using fresh beans, add 2 tbs. of water. You don't need to add water for frozen beans. Add grated coconut.
- Press CANCEL and cover the lid, keep the vent in the sealing position and pressure cook on high for 0 mins. When the Instant Pot beeps, release pressure by moving the vent carefully to the venting position. Remove the lid and mix well.
- Serve hot with steamed rice and curry.

Easy Dal Fry

Servings: 2 Calories: 428kcal Course: Soup Prep Time: 15 mins Cook Time: 30 mins Total Time: 45 mins

Ingredients

1 cup red lentils or a cup of split pigeon peas
3 to 3.5 cups of water
1 inch ginger minced
1/2 tsp turmeric
3/4 tsp salt or to taste

Tempering:

1 tsp oil
1/2 tsp cumin seeds
1/2 tsp mustard seeds optional
1 -2 bay leaves
2 cloves
a pinch of asafetida hing optional
1/2 red onion finely chopped
4 cloves garlic finely chopped
2 green chilies chopped or sliced
1/2 to 1 tsp Garam Masala
1/4 to 1/2 tsp cayenne red chili powder
1/2 tsp dry mango powder amchur or add lime juice to taste
1 tbsp vegan butter

1/2 cup chopped cilantro for garnish

Directions

- Cook the lentils in Instant Pot until done to preference. Continue to simmer the lentils over low heat while you make the tempering. Fold in the ginger, turmeric and salt. Manual for 1 to 2 mins. NATURAL RELEASE.
- Make the Tempering: Heat oil in a skillet over medium heat. When hot, add cumin and mustard seeds and let them start to change color. Add bay leaves and cloves and cook until they get fragrant.
- Add asafetida and mix in. Add onion, garlic, chile and cook until translucent.
- Add this tempering to the simmering lentils. Add garam masala, amchur and cayenne and vegan butter.
- Taste and adjust salt and heat. Add cayenne or lemon juice if needed. Fold in chopped tomatoes or chopped baby spinach at this point. Add cilantro and mix in.
- Serve hot as a soup or with rice and roasted veggies.

Rajma |Kidney Beans Curry
This popular comfort food is best enjoyed with steamed basmati rice.

Servings: 5 Calories: 180 kcal Course: Main Course Prep Time: 10 mins Cook Time: 30 mins Soak Beans: 8 hrs Total Time: 9 hrs

Ingredients

1 cup Red Kidney Beans Dry (Rajma) soaked overnight
1 tablespoon Light Olive Oil or Ghee
1 tsp. Cumin Seed
1 small onion finely chopped
1 tbs. ginger garlic paste ½ inch ginger + 3 cloves garlic
2 green chillies whole or de-seeded (Optional)
2 medium tomatoes pureed, OR, 1 cup Crushed Tomatoes
1.5 cups water

Spices

1 tsp. salt adjust to taste
½ tsp. Turmeric Powder
1 tsp. Garam Masala
2 tsp.s Ground Coriander

1 tsp. Roasted Ground Cumin
½ tsp Red Chili Powder

Garnish

2 tbs. chopped cilantro for garnish

Directions

- Prep: If using dry kidney beans, rinse and soak them overnight. Drain them before use. Chop onions and crush ginger-garlic. You can do that by pulsing them together in a mini food processor. Puree tomatoes if using fresh.
- Turn the instant pot on SAUTE mode, adjust to more. When the display reads 'hot add oil or ghee and cumin seeds.
- When the cumin seeds begin to sizzle (a few seconds), add chopped onions, green chilies and crushed ginger-garlic. Saute for 3-5 mins, till onions soften.
- Add crushed tomatoes, salt, turmeric, garam masala, cumin, coriander, cayenne and paprika. Saute for 1 minute.
- Add drained and rinsed kidney beans to the pot. Add fresh water and stir.
- Close the lid and set the valve to SEALING position. Cook on Bean/Chili or Pressure Cook mode for 30 mins.
- After the cooking time is done, wait for the pressure to RELEASE NATURALLY (NPR). Open the lid after the pin drops and garnish with chopped cilantro.
- Serve warm with white or brown basmati rice.

Bottle Gourd Kurma Recipe

A healthy curry recipe made with the bottle gourd aka Lauki cooked together in an aromatic spicy kurma or korma masala made of coconut, cashews and other spices.

Servings: 4 Calories: 120kcal Course: curry, Main Course Prep Time: 10 mins Cook Time: 15 mins Total Time: 25 mins

Ingredients

1 small lauki aka bottle gourd peeled and diced (about 2 cups)
1 tablespoon oil
1 tsp. cumin (jeera) seeds
1 tablespoon ginger garlic paste
2 green chiles finely chopped
1 small onion finely chopped

1 large tomato finely chopped
½ tsp. turmeric powder
½ tsp. red chilli powder
1 tsp. coriander powder
½ tsp. garam masala
¾ cup water
 salt to taste
2 tbs. cilantro/coriander leaves
1 tablespoon lemon juice

For Grinding

¼ cup fresh or frozen coconut
6-8 cashews or 2 tsp. of poppy seeds
1 inch cinnamon
2 cloves
1 tsp. saunf (fennel seeds) optional

Directions

- Wash Bottle Gourd, peel the skin, deseed if any and cut into ½ inch pieces.
- Grind coconut, cashews, cloves, cinnamon to a smooth paste.
- Press SAUTE on Instant Pot. Add oil in to the POT.Once oil is hot add cumin seeds and let them crackle.
- Next add ginger garlic paste and green chilles, Saute for few seconds.
- Add onions and saute until onions turn light brown.
- Next add chopped tomatoes, spices like red chilli powder, garam masala powder, coriander powder, garam masala powder and cook till they turn soft.
- Then add the water and deglaze the pot to remove any bits stuck to the bottom of the pot.
- Add in the diced bottle gourd, ground coconut-cashew paste, salt and mix well.
- Close the lid on the pot, and turn pressure valve to SEALING position.
- Set the pot to MANUAL/PRESSURE COOK (High Pressure) and set timer to 3 mins.
- Once the pot beeps, Do a NATURAL PRESSURE RELEASE.
- Remove lid away from you, add lime juice and garnish with cilantro.Mix well.
- Serve with hot with pooris, chapatis, roti & parathas.

Red Lentil Butternut Squash Curry

Calories: 212kcal Servings: 4 Course: MainCuisine Prep Time: 15 mins Cook Time: 10 mins Total Time: 15 mins

Ingredients

1 tsp oil
1/2 tsp mustard seeds
4 cloves of garlic finely chopped
1/2 medium onion finely chopped
1 inch ginger finely chopped
1 hot green chili finely chopped
1/2 tsp turmeric
1/2 tsp garam masala or curry powder
1/4 tsp black pepper or cayenne, or both
1 large tomato chopped
12 oz butternut squash or pumpkin raw, peeled and cubed or frozen
1/3 cup red lentils
14 oz can of coconut milk
1/2 cup of water
salt
3-4 oz of baby spinach
lime juice and cilantro for garnish

Directions

- Start the Instant Pot on SAUTÉ. Add the oil and once it has heated, add the mustard seeds and wait for them to sputter or change color. Add the chopped onion, garlic, ginger, chili and a pinch of salt. COOK for 2 mins.
- Add the spices and mix well. Add the tomatoes and a quarter cup of water and cook for 2 mins stirring occasionally to avoid sticking.
- Add the butternut squash or pumpkin, coconut milk, lentils, water and salt. Mix well to combine and pick up the tomato from the bottom of the pot. Close the lid and PRESSURE COOK for 4 mins. Carefully QUICK RELEASE the pressure slowly once cooking time is done.
- Open the lid and fold in the spinach and mix thoroughly. Taste and adjust the amount of salt, heat and flavor. Add a good dash of lime juice.
- Garnish with pepper flakes or cilantro.
- Serve over rice or flat bread or with fresh dinner rolls.

Vegetable Korma| Navratan Korma
This is a mildly spiced, slightly sweet, creamy based delicious Indian curry.

Servings: 6 Calories: 365kcal Course: Side Dish Prep Time : 10 mins Cook Time: 10 mins Total Time : 20 mins

Ingredients

2 medium onion (about 1.5 cups)
10-12 cashew nuts
3 garlic cloves
1 inch ginger
1 cup carrots cut into ½ inch pieces
1 cup cauliflower large florets
½ cup green beans cut into ½ inch pieces
1 cup potato cut into ½ inch pieces
½ cup green peas
2 tbs. oil
1 bay leaf
1 tsp. cumin (jeera) seeds
¼ tsp. turmeric powder
½ tsp. red chilli powder
1 tsp. coriander powder
1 tsp. garam masala powder
1.5 cups water
salt to taste
1 cup paneer
¼ cup cashew nuts
¼ cup raisins
¼ cup pineapple chunks
½ cup cream or cashew cream or coconut cream
1 tbs. kasuri methi (dried fenugreek leaves) (optional)

Directions

- To a blender add the onions, Cashew nuts, garlic and ginger. Blend to a smooth paste without adding any water. Set aside.
- Press SAUTE mode on Instant Pot. Add oil and once it's hot add cashews, raisins and pineapple chunks. Saute for 2 mins, Once the cashews are golden brown, take the cashews, raisins and pineapple out and set aside.
- Adding pineapple is optional, so if you dont like the sweetness in the dish skip it.
- Next add the bay leaf, cumin(jeera) seeds and let the cumin crackle.
- Next add the onion cashew paste and saute for 3-4 mins or until onion mixture turns light brown in color.

- Then add the mixed vegetables.
- Add the red chilli powder, turmeric powder, coriander powder, water and combine well.
- Close the lid on the pot. Set the pot to MANUAL/PRESSURE COOK (High Pressure) and set timer to 2 mins
- Once the pot beeps. Do a QUICK RELEASE(QR)
- Add the fried cashews, raisins, pineapple, cream, kasuri methi (dried fenugreek leaves) ,garam masala and stir well.
- Adjust consistency at this stage, if curry is thick add some more water or milk or cream.
- Serve with hot with pooris, chapatis, roti & parathas.

Tadka dal | One Pot Lentil Soup

Servings: 4 Calories: 201kcal Course: main coursePrep time: 5 mins Cook time: 15 mins Total time: 20 mins

Ingredients

2 tbs. coconut or olive oil
1 tsp. mustard seeds
1 sprig of curry leaves
2-3 dried red chilies (optional)
a pinch of asafoetida
2 garlic cloves chopped
½ cup finely chopped onions
½ cup finely diced tomatoes
2 green chili peppers chopped
½ tsp. turmeric powder
salt to taste
1 cup toor dal / tuvar dal (split pigeon peas)
3 tbs. finely chopped cilantro / coriander leaves for garnishing

Directions

- Add oil to the steel insert of the Instant Pot and press the SAUTE function. Press the Adjust button to move the selection to "low" and wait till the display reads "Hot." Add mustard seeds and as they begin to splutter add curry leaves, dried chilies, asafoetida, and garlic.
- After 10 seconds or so add cut tomatoes, onions, green chilies, turmeric powder, and salt. Fry it for a min.

- Wash the dal and add it to the steel insert along with 2.5 cups of water. Press "Warm / Cancel" button and then select "Pressure Cook." Adjust the time to 15 mins and set the pressure selection to high. Cover the Instant Pot lid and lock it.
- Make sure the vent is at SEALING position. Allow to NATURALLY RELEASE PRESSURE. Return the vent to the venting position, open the Instant pot lid and garnish it with coriander leaves before serving.

Aloo Methi | Potatoes with Fenugreek Leaves

Servings: 3 Calories: 235 kcal Course: Side Dish Prep Time: 15 mins Cook Time: 15 mins Total Time: 30 mins

Ingredients

3 tbs. oil
1 tsp. cumin seeds
1 tsp. black mustard seeds
1 ½ pounds unpeeled baby potatoes, cut in half

Spices

1 ¼ tsp. salt
1 tsp. amchur dried mango powder
1 tsp. black salt
½ tsp. black pepper
¼ tsp. cayenne
½ cup frozen or thawed onion masala
¼ cup water
1 cup dried fenugreek leaves (kasoori methi)

Directions

- Press SAUTÉ and add oil to the pot. Once the oil is hot, add the cumin and mustard seeds. When the cumin begins to brown, add the potatoes and spices and mix well.
- Add the onion masala and water to the pot.
- Secure the lid, close the pressure valve and cook for 4 mins at high pressure.
- QUICK RELEASE PRESSURE.
- Add the dried fenugreek leaves to the pot and mix well. The leaves will absorb any remaining liquid in the pot.

Smoky Tofu Quinoa Biryani
A flavorful and hearty one-pot dish!

Serving Size: 1 Calories: 428kcal Course: Main course Prep Time: 5 Mins Cook Time: 25 Mins Total Time: 30 Mins

Ingredients

Marinated Tofu

7 ounces extra firm tofu
1/2 cup non-dairy yogurt
1 tbsp ginger paste
2 cloves garlic, minced
1 tbsp freshly chopped cilantro
1 tbsp freshly chopped mint
2 tbsp lime juice
1 tbsp garam masala
1 tsp dried fenugreek leaves
1/2 tsp ground chili powder
1/4 tsp smoked paprika
1/8 tsp cinnamon
1/2 tsp salt
1/4 tsp liquid smoke (optional)

Quinoa Biryani

2 tbsp oil
2 onions, finely sliced
1 tbsp oil
1 red bell pepper, diced
1 and 1/2 cup quinoa
2 and 1/3 cup water
2 tbsp raisins
2 green cardamom pods, crushed
1 cinnamon stick
1 bay leaf
1/4 tsp salt

Directions

- Cut the tofu into 1-inch cubes.

- In a large bowl, combine the non-dairy yogurt, ginger paste, minced garlic, cilantro, mint, lime juice, garam masala, fenugreek, ground chili, smoked paprika, cinnamon, salt, and liquid smoke. Mix until well combined. Add the tofu and stir to coat with the marinade.
- Cover the bowl with plastic film and let marinate in the refrigerator for at least 1 hour, or preferably overnight.
- Put on the Instant Pot on SAUTÉ mode. Once hot, add the oil and onions. Fry the onions until they turn golden brown and caramelize, about 7-10 minutes. Remove the onions from the Instant Pot, transfer to a plate and set aside.
- Heat another tablespoon of oil in the Instant Pot. Add the marinated tofu and red bell peppers, and SAUTÉ for about 5 minutes, stirring regularly to prevent the tofu from sticking. Turn the sauté mode off.
- Add the caramelized onions, quinoa, water, raisins, cardamom pods, cinnamon stick, bay leaf, and salt on top of the sautéed tofu. Close the lid and pressure cook on manual for 1 minute. After 1 minute, let the PRESSURE RELEASE NATURALLY, this should take around 10 minutes. Remove the lid and fluff the quinoa with a fork.
- Serve immediately topped with fresh cilantro, lime, and/or a dollop of non-dairy yogurt.

Punjabi Kala Chana | Black Chickpeas Curry

This is a mildly spiced black chickpeas curry, a simple everyday Punjabi curry, made in an onion-tomato gravy with ginger and garlic.

Servings: 4 Calories: 250 Course: Main Course Prep Time: 10 mins Cook Time: 40 mins Total Time: 50 mins

Ingredients

1 cup Black Chickpeas (Kala Chana) 250 ml
3 cup Water for soaking
1 tbsp Oil
1 tsp Cumin seeds (Jeera)
1 Onion medium diced (about 1 cup)
2 Tomato medium chopped (about 1 cup)
1 Green Chili Pepper minced (optional)
1Ginger minced (or 1 tsp. Ginger paste)
5 cloves Garlic minced (or 1 tsp. Garlic paste)
2 cups Water for cooking
1 tsp Dry Mango powder (Amchur) (can be replaced with lemon juice)
Cilantro to garnish

Spices

2 tsp Coriander powder
½ tsp Garam masala
½ tsp Cayenne or Red chili powder
¼ tsp Ground Turmeric
1 tsp Salt

Directions

- Wash chickpeas and soak for 6 hours or overnight in 3 cups of water. The chickpeas will increase in size when they are soaked.
- Start the instant pot in sauté mode and let it heat. Add oil, cumin seeds to it.
- When the cumin seeds start to splutter, add chopped onion, ginger, garlic and chili pepper. Sauté for 3 mins.
- Add chopped tomatoes and spices. Stir and sauté for another 2 mins.
- Drain the soaking water from kala chana. Add kala chana and 2 cups of fresh water to the instant pot.
- Change the instant pot setting to bean/chili mode. This will automatically set the timer to 30 mins.
- When the instant pot beeps, let the PRESSURE RELEASE NATURALLY (NPR). If the pin has not dropped after 20 mins, release the pressure manually.
- Open the instant pot and add amchur (dry mango powder) to it. Stir well for a minute.
- Garnish with cilantro. Serve with rice or roti.

Ven Pongal

This Indian breakfast is a great way to start your day.

Servings: 6 Calories: 254kcal Course: Breakfast Prep Time: 5 Minscook Time: 15 Mins total Time: 20 Mins

Ingredients

1 cup sona masoori rice
½ cup moong dal
3 tbs. ghee or coconut oil
1 tsp. cumin seeds
½ tsp. whole black peppercorns

1 tbs. grated ginger
a pinch of asafoetida
1 sprig of curry leaves or kadipatta around 8-10
8-10 cashews halved
1-2 green chilies finely chopped
1 tsp. salt or as needed
5 cups water

Directions

- Wash and rinse the dal and rice using a colander and set aside.
- Set the Instant Pot to 'SAUTE' mode and adjust the setting to 'More'. When the display reads 'Hot', add ghee.
- Once the ghee heats up, add cumin seeds and black peppercorns. As the cumin seeds start to splutter, add curry leaves, asafoetida, green chilies, ginger, and cashews.
- When the cashews turn golden brown, add rice and dal and mix well. Saute them for a minute or two before adding water and salt. Mix well. Close the vent and set it to the sealing position.
- Pressure cook under high pressure or use the Porridge mode and set it for 10 mins.
- Once cooking is complete, allow the pressure to RELEASE NATURALLY before opening the lid.
- Mix well and serve hot with sambar and coconut chutney.
- The next step would be the tempering process - cumin seeds are added to hot ghee and when it starts to splutter cashews, curry leaves, asafoetida, green chilies, peppercorns are added to it.
- Saute them before pouring it over Pongal.

Black Eyed Peas Curry |Indian Lobia Masala

This is a popular healthy Punjabi curry which is deliciously made using onion-tomato base and few spices.

Servings: 4 Calories : 129.9kcal Course: Dinner, Main Course Prep Time : 15 mins
Cook Time : 20 mins Total Time : 35 mins

Ingredients

1 cup black eyes peas soaked in water for 4 or more hours (it will double up to 2 cups)
1 tbs. oil
1 tsp. jeera (cumin) seeds

1 medium onion
1 tbs. ginger-garlic paste finely chopped
2 green chillies chopped
2 medium tomatoes
2 cups water for cooking
1 tbs. lemon juice
2 tbs. coriander leaves/cilantro for garnish

Spices

½ tsp. turmeric (haldi powder)
1 tsp. red chilli (mirchi powder)
1 tsp. coriander (dhaniya powder)
1 tsp. garam masala powder
salt to taste

Directions

- Soak the black eyed peas in abundant water for 4 or more hours so they are all submerged. When you are ready to cook, drain the water.
- Grind/Blend 2 tomatoes to make a puree.
- Press SAUTE mode on Instant Pot. Add oil in to the POT.Once POT is hot add cumin(jeera) seeds, let them splutter.
- Add onions, green chillies, ginger-garlic paste and saute until onions turn light brown (approximately 5-6 mins).
- Next add tomato puree or finely chopped tomatoes and cook the mixture for another 2-3 mins.
- Then add soaked black eyed peas, red chilli powder, turmeric powder,coriander powder,salt and mix well.
- Then add water and give a stir.
- Close the lid on the pot. Set the pot to MANUAL/PRESSURE COOK (High Pressure) and set timer to 12 mins for firmer beans & 14 mins for softer beans.
- Do a NATURAL PRESSURE RELEASE(NPR) for atleast 10 mins.
- Remove lid away from you, add garam masala powder, lime juice and garnish with cilantro.Mix well.
- Serve with hot with rice, pooris, chapatis, roti & parathas.

Mix Vegetable Kurma

This is a popular Indian curry in which vegetables are cooked in a creamy and aromatic gravy of yogurt, coconut and cashew nuts based paste and sautéed onion and tomato along with few spices.

Servings: 4 Calories: 145 Course: Main Course, Side Dish Prep Time: 10 mins Cook Time : 10 mins Total Time : 20 mins

Ingredients

½ cup grated coconut fresh or frozen
6-7 cashewnuts
1 tbs. fried gram (roasted chana dal)
1 inch ginger
2 large garlic
1 green chilli
2 cardamom
2 cloves
1 inch cinnamon stick
1 tsp. saunf(fennel)
1 tsp. coriander seeds or 1 tsp. coriander powder
½ tsp. jeera seeds(cumin) or ½ tsp. of jeera (cumin) powder
water for grinding
4-5 cups mix vegetables (carrot, beans, cauliflower, potato, peas)
1 cup onion finely chopped
½ cup tomato finely chopped
1 tsp. red chilli powder
½ tsp. turmeric powder
½ tsp. garam masala powder
1 tbs. curd (yogurt) or vegan yogurt, optional
salt as per taste
1.5 cups water as required
2 tbs. oil
1 tablespoon coriander leaves (cilantro)
1 tablespoon lime juice

Directions

- To a blender add all these ingredients (coconut, cashew nuts, fried gram, ginger, garlic, green chilli, cardamom cloves, cinnamon stick, saunf(fennel), coriander seeds or powder, jeera seeds(cumin) or powder). Add ¼ cup of water and blend to a smooth paste. Set aside.
- Press SAUTE mode on Instant Pot. Add oil in to the POT.
- Once POT is hot add Bay leaf, onions and saute until onions turn light brown for 2 mins.

- Next add chopped tomatoes and cook till they turn soft.
- Add the prepared coconut-cashew paste, red chilli powder, turmeric powder, garam masala, curd(yogurt) and Stir continuously for 2 mins until raw smell disappears.
- Now add the veggies, salt and water and combine well.
- Close the lid on the pot, and turn pressure valve to SEALING position.
- Set the pot to MANUAL/PRESSURE COOK (High Pressure) and set timer to 3 mins
- Do a QUICK RELEASE(QR)
- Remove lid away from you, add lime juice and garnish with cilantro. Mix well.
- Serve with hot with pooris, chapatis, roti & parathas.

Rice Pudding / Kheer

Servings: 6 Calories: 305 kcal Course: Dessert Prep Time: 5 mins Cook Time: 30 mins Total Time: 50 mins

Ingredients

Kheer

½ cup Basmati rice or Jasmine,
⅓ cup assorted chopped nuts
½ tsp. ground cardamom
¼ cup water
5 cups milk can use whole milk
½ cup + 2 tbsp sugar

Optional Ingredients

2 tbs. raisins
1 tablespoon unsweetened flaked coconut
½ tsp. saffron

Directions

Rinse rice 2-3 times, or till water runs clear. Soak in water till you arrange everything together. Chop nuts to your liking. Crush cardamom if using fresh.

Turn on SAUTE. Add water. Now add the milk. This prevents the milk from scorching in the bottom of the pan.

Add sugar.

Add nuts and rinsed rice, and give it a stir. As soon as the milk comes to a simmer, hit Cancel.

Set Porridge mode for 20 mins, on sealing mode. Once the cook time is done, let the PRESSURE RELEASE NATURALLY for at least 15 mins, followed by QUICK RELEASE of any remaining pressure.

Open the lid after the pin drops. Using the back of your ladle, mash the rice against the sides of the pot. Alternatively, use a potato masher. Mashing makes the rice pudding naturally creamy.

Stir in ground cardamom. Garnish with more nuts if you like and enjoy hot or chill in the refrigerator for a few hours.

Cabbage Peas Stir Fry|Patta Gobi Matar

A very delicious side dish recipe prepared with cabbage, green peas and a mix of spices.

Servings: 3 Calories: 165 Course: Main Course, Side Dish Prep Time : 5 mins Cook Time : 10 mins Total Time : 15 mins

Ingredients

4 cups cabbage slice into fine long shreds
½ fresh/frozen cup peas
1 tbs. coconut oil
½ tsp. cumin seeds (jeera)
2 green chilies finely chopped
1 tsp. ginger minced
½ tsp. ground turmeric (haldi)
¼ tsp. red chilli powder or cayenne pepper (lal mirch)
1 tsp. coriander powder
½ tsp. garam masala
¼ tsp. sugar (optional)
2-3 tbs. water
 1 tsp. lemon juice or [¼ tsp. dry mango powder
2 tbsp chopped cilantro/coriander leaves (optional)
salt to taste

Directions

- Press SAUTE mode on Instant Pot. Add oil in to the POT.Once hot, add cumin seeds, let them splutter. Next add minced ginger, green chili. Saute for 20 secs .

- Add shredded cabbage, green peas, turmeric powder, coriander powder, sugar, salt, water and mix well. Make sure to scrap of any spice if sticking to the pot.
- Close the lid on the pot, and turn pressure valve to SEALING position. Press CANCEL button on Instant Pot.
- Set the pot to MANUAL/PRESSURE COOK (High Pressure) and set timer to 1 minute. When the instant pot beeps,Do a QUICK RELEASE(QR)
- Remove lid away from you, sprinkle garam masala and lemon juice, Mix well. If there is any water, change the setting to saute mode and get it to your desired consistency.
- Serve with hot with chapatis, roti & parathas.

Butter chicken with soy curls & chickpeas.

Servings: 3 Calories: 318kcal Course: Entree, Main Course Prep Time: 10 mins Cook Time: 35 mins Total Time: 45 mins

Ingredients

3 large ripe tomatoes or can diced tomatoes
4 cloves of garlic
1/2 inch cube of ginger
1 hot or mild green chile
3/4 cup water
½ to 1 tsp garam masala
½ tsp paprika or kashmiri chili powder
¼ to ½ tsp cayenne
 salt
1 cup dry, not rehydrated soy curls
1 cup cooked chickpeas
Cashew cream made with with ¼ cup soaked cashews blended with ½ cup water
1/2 tsp or more garam masala
1/2 tsp or more sugar or sweetener
1 tsp kasoori methi - dried fenugreek leaves or add a 1/4 tsp ground mustard
1/2 moderately hot green chile finely chopped, or 2 tbsp finely chopped green bell pepper
1/2 tsp minced or finely chopped ginger
1/4 cup cilantro for garnish

Directions

- Blend the tomatoes, garlic, ginger, chile with water until smooth.

- Add pureed tomato mixture to the Instant pot. Add soy curls, chickpeas, spices and salt. Close the lid and PRESS MANUAL/PRESSURE COOK for 8 to 10 mins. QUICK RELEASE after 10 mins.
- Start the IP on SAUTE, add the cashew cream, garam masala, sweetener and fenugreek leaves and mix in. Bring to a boil, taste and adjust salt, heat, sweet. Add more cayenne and salt if needed. Fold in the chopped green chile, ginger and cilantro and press CANCEL (take off heat).
- At this point you can add some vegan butter or oil for additional buttery flavor. Serve hot over rice or with flatbread or Naan.

Curd Rice | Thayir Sadam

The delicate and mild flavored curd rice is a befitting finale to a sumptuous spicy meal.

Servings: 8 Calories: 255kcal Course: main course Prep Time: 5 Mins cook Time: 10 Mins resting Time: 15 Mins total Time: 30 Mins

Ingredients

2 cups basmati rice
2 cups yogurt fresh
1 cup milk
1 cup grated cucumber
2 Indian or Thai green chilies chopped finely
1 inch-piece ginger finely grated

For tempering

1 tbs. oil or ghee
1 tsp. mustard seeds
¼ tsp. asafoetida
1 tsp. urad dal washed and rinsed
2 whole dried red chili halved
A sprig of curry leaves

Directions

- Cook rice with twice the amount of water either over the stovetop or in Instant Pot.
- Whisk yogurt with milk till they are well combined. Add grated cucumber, green chilies, salt, grated ginger and mix well.

- Add the yogurt mixture to rice and mash well using your fingers or the back of a ladle.
- Add oil or ghee to the tadka pan kept over medium-heat.
- When the oil is hot, add mustard seeds and asafoetida. Once the mustard seeds start to sputter, add urad, red chili and a sprig of curry leaves.
- Let them sizzle for about 10 seconds and then pour this mixture over curd rice mixture. Garnish with cilantro and mix well.
- Serve immediately accompanied by pickle and/or papads.

Carrot Halwa | Gajar Ka Halwa

Servings: 8 Calories: 301 kcal Course: Dessert Prep Time: 10 mins Cook Time: 2 mins Total Time: 35 mins

Ingredients

4 tbs. ghee or unsalted butter
¼ cup cashews and almonds chopped
6 cups carrots grated
1 cup milk
½ tsp. saffron optional, but recommended
¾ cup sugar
1¼ cups Nonfat Milk Powder
½ tsp. green cardamom powder
1 tablespoon almonds chopped for garnish (optional)

Directions

- Prep: Wash, peel and grate carrots. Chop cashews and almonds and keep aside.
- Turn the instant pot on SAUTE mode, when it displays "hot", add ghee or butter. Add chopped nuts and carrots and saute for 2 mins. This prevents the carrots from turning mushy later.
- Add milk, saffron and sugar, stir well. Wait till the milk comes to a simmer. Close lid and cook on MANUAL/PRESSURE COOK for 2 mins. Set the valve to Sealing position in DUO.
- After pressure cooking is done, MANUALLY RELEASE PRESSURE (QR) and open the lid after the pin drops. Turn on SAUTE (high). Add milk powder and stir. Cook off the liquid, stirring every few mins. This takes around 10-15 mins.
- Add cardamom powder and stir. Garnish with chopped almonds (optional)
- Serve warm!

Easy Aromatic Jeera Rice | Cumin rice

Servings: 4 Calories: 211kcal Course: Main Course Prep Time: 5 Mins Cook Time: 5 Mins total Time: 10 Mins

Ingredients

1 cup Basmati rice
water
1 tbs. ghee
2 tsp.s cumin seeds
1-2 green chilies finely chopped
1 cinnamon stick 3-inch long
1-2 Indian bay leaves
salt as needed

Directions

- Add rice to a medium-deep saucepan and fill it with water till the rice is completely covered.
- Wash the rice
- Change the water couple of times till the water runs clear. Drain the water and add 3 cups of water to the rice. Let the rice soak for 30 mins.
- Drain the rice and set aside.
- Add ghee to the steel insert of the Instant Pot and press the SAUTE function. Press the Adjust button to move the selection to "Normal" and wait until the display reads "Hot."
- Once the ghee is hot, add cumin seeds and once it starts sizzling, add green chilies, bay leaves, and cinnamon stick. Fry it for about 10-15 seconds and then add rice.
- Saute the rice for about 1-2 mins before adding salt and 1 cup of water.
- Press the "Warm / Cancel" button and then select "Pressure Cook." or "Manual" depending on your model.
- Adjust the time to 5 mins and set the pressure selection at low. Cover the Instant Pot lid and lock it. Make sure the vent is at sealing position.
- Once the cooking cycle completes, the Instant Pot will switch to the Warm cycle. Press the Warm/Cancel button and carefully RELEASE PRESSURE. Open the lid and let the steam escape.
- Cover the Instant Pot and let the rice rest undisturbed for 5 mins. Fluff the rice gently with a fork, sprinkle chopped coriander leaves and serve immediately.

Zucchini Dal Recipe
An easy dal with masoor dal (red lentils), zucchini, tomatoes, indian spices and
cooked with pot-in-pot rice

Servings: 4 Calories: 214kcal Course: Main Course Prep Time : 10 mins Cook Time :
15 mins Total Time : 25 mins

Ingredients

1 cup masoor dal (red lentils)
2-3 cups zucchini chopped into 1.5 inch pieces
1 tbs. ghee or coconut oil
1 tsp. cumin seeds(jeera)
1 pinch asafetida (hing)
2 green chillies split into halve
1 tbs. ginger and garlic paste
1 small onion finely chopped
1 large tomato finely chopped
salt to taste
3 cups water
2 tablespoon cilantro/coriander leaves chopped
½ lemon juice

Dry Spices:

½ tsp. turmeric powder (haldi)
1 tsp. red chilli powder
1 tsp. coriander powder
½ tsp. garam masala powder
For Basmati Rice
1 cup basmati rice
1.5 cups water
a pinch salt (optional)

Directions

- Press Saute mode on Instant Pot. Add oil and once it's hot add cumin seeds. Let them crackle.
- Add ginger garlic paste, asafetida, green chili and saute for 15-20 secs.
- Then add chopped onion. Saute till onions turn light brown in color.

- Add tomatoes along with dry spices turmeric powder, red chili powder, coriander powder, garam masala powder and cook till tomatoes turn soft, takes 2-3 mins.
- Then add diced zucchini, rinsed lentils or dal, salt, water and give a stir. Adjust spices at this stage. No need to soak the dal for this recipe.
- Once you add all ingredients for Zucchini Dal in the instant pot, place the trivet and then the bowl of rice with water. This way they will both cook together
- Close the lid on the pot, and turn pressure valve to SEALING position. Set the pot to MANUAL/PRESSURE COOK (High Pressure) and increase timer to 5 mins.
- Once the pot beeps, let it release the pressure naturally for 10 mins.
- Add cilantro and lime juice, mix well serve hot with boiled rice, quinoa or roti.

Palak Paneer|Spinach and Cottage Cheese Curry

This is a dish consisting of palak (spinach) and paneer (cottage cheese) in a thick curry sauce based on pureed spinach, onion, tomatoes and spices

Servings: 4 Calories: 254 Course: Gravy, Side Dish Prep Time: 10 mins Cook Time: 10 mins Total Time: 20 mins

Ingredients

10 oz spinach(palak)
1 cup paneer (cottage cheese)
2 tablespoon oil or ghee
1 tsp. cumin (jeera) seeds
1 medium onion finely chopped
½ inch ginger minced
3 garlic cloves minced
2 green chillies finely chopped
1 large tomato finely chopped (about 1 cup)
½ tsp. turmeric powder
½ tsp. red chilli powder
1 tsp. coriander powder
1 tsp. garam masala
salt to taste
½ cup water
1 tbs. fresh cream or cashew cream (optional)
1 tbs. kasuri methi (dried fenugreek leaves) (optional)

Directions

- Press SAUTE on Instant Pot. Add oil in to the POT.
- Once oil is hot add cumin seeds, let the cumin splutter then add onions, minced ginger and garlic, green chili and fry until onions turn light brown.
- Next add diced tomato, red chili powder, turmeric powder, coriander powder, salt and cook for 1-2 mins.
- Add water and deglaze the pot. Next add in the baby spinach.
- Close the lid on the pot, and turn pressure valve to SEALING position.
- Set the pot to MANUAL/PRESSURE COOK (High Pressure) and set timer to 2 Mins.If using frozen spinach then set timer to 1 Minute.
- Once the pot beeps, Do a QUICK RELEASE (QR).
- Blend the ingredients in the pot to a creamy texture using an immersion blender. If you dont have immersion blender then take the mixture out, cool it and then blend in a regular blender and add the mixture back to the instant pot.
- Add garam masala, kasuri methi and paneer and mix well. You can also add some fresh cream or cashew cream. No need to boil/saute again after adding paneer. Let it sit for 5 mins
- Serve it with your favorite Indian bread variety or rice.

Black eyed peas curry | chawli / lobia masala
A simple yet flavorful curry, healthy and satisfying.

Servings: 4 Calories: 223kcal Course: Main course Prep Time: 10 Mins Cook Time: 30 Mins Total Time: 40 Mins

Ingredients

3 tbs. oil olive or coconut
1.5 cups chopped onion
4-5 cloves garlic cloves minced
¼ tsp. grated ginger
1.5 cups chopped tomato
salt to taste
1 tsp. cumin powder
1 tsp. coriander powder
½ tsp. red chili powder
1-2 green chilies cut lengthwise
1 cup chawli black-eyed peas, soaked overnight
1 tablespoon powdered jaggery
¼ tsp. tamarind paste or ½ tablespoon lime juice
¼ tablespoon dried methi leaves for garnishing

Cilantro / Coriander leaves for garnishing

Directions

- Add oil to the steel insert of the Instant Pot and press the SAUTE function. Press the Adjust button to move the selection to "Normal" and wait till the display reads "Hot." and then add onions. Fry the onions till they turn soft and translucent (approximately 6-8 mins).
- Add ginger and garlic and saute it with the onions for a minute or so. Add tomatoes and continue frying them till they are soft and mushy, (approximately 10 mins).
- Add chili powder, coriander, and cumin powder along with salt and stir it in. Fry this mixture for about 5 mins and then grind this onion-tomato gravy to a fine paste along with green chilies. Press "Warm/Cancel" to switch off Instant Pot.
- Add the onion-tomato paste in the steel insert of the Instant Pot and press the Saute function. Press the ADJUST button to move the selection to "Normal." Let the paste cook for 5 mins and then add black-eyed peas along with 2 cups of water (1.5 cups of water for a thicker gravy).
- Press "Warm / Cancel" button and then select "Pressure Cook." Adjust the time to 15 mins and set the pressure selection at high. Cover the Instant Pot lid and lock it. Make sure the vent is at SEALING position.
- Wait until the vent returns to the venting position and then open the lid and then stir in garam masala powder, lemon juice, jaggery and dried methi leaves.
- Garnish it with coriander leaves and serve hot with rice or roti.

Eggplant Sweet Potato Lentil Curry

Servings: 4 Calories: 200kcal Course: Main Course, Soup Prep Time: 15 mins Cook Time: 35 mins Total Time: 50 mins

Ingredients

3/4 cup lentils
1 tsp oil
1/2 onion chopped
4 cloves of garlic chopped
an inch of ginger chopped
1/2 or 1 hot green chile chopped
1/4 tsp turmeric
1/2 to 1 tsp garam masala

1/2 tsp ground cumin or ground coriander
15 oz tomatoes (2 medium tomatoes, chopped)
1 cup chopped eggplant
1 cup cubed sweet potatoes
3/4 tsp salt
2 cups water
a big handful of spinach
cayenne and lemon/lime to taste
pepper flakes for garnish

Directions

- Soak the lentils if you havent already and get the ingredients ready, Switch the IP to SAUTE. Add oil and let it get hot.
- Add onion, garlic, ginger, chile and a pinch of salt. Cook for 2 to 3 mins, stir frequently.
- Add spices and mix in. Add tomatoes and cook for 4 to 5 mins. Mash larger pieces. Add the veggies, salt, lentils and water and mix in.
- Close the lid, to SEALING, and cook on MANUAL for 11 to 12 mins (on HIGH PRESSURE). Let the PRESSURE RELEASE NATURALLY.
- Fold in spinach, cayenne and lemon./lime. Let it sit for 2 mins or saute for 2 mins. Adjust consistency if needed by adding a bit more water or non dairy milk for creamier and mix in. Taste and adjust salt, spices.
- Serve with flatbread or rice/cooked grains or as a soup with crackers.

Mushroom Masala|Mushroom Curry

This is an easy and delicious restaurant style Indian Curry made with onions, tomato, mushrooms, peas and spices.

Servings: 4 Calories: 180kcal Course: curry, Main Course Prep Time : 15 mins Cook Time : 15 mins Total Time : 30 mins

Ingredients

10-12 cashews
8 oz organic white mushrooms sliced (about 2 cups)
½ cup green peas (optional)
1.5 tablespoon coconut oil
1 medium red onion diced (about 1 cup)
1 inch ginger chopped
3 large garlic cloves

1 green chilli
2 large tomatoes diced (about 1.5 cups)
½ tsp. red chili powder
½ tsp. garam masala
¼ tsp. turmeric powder
1 tsp. coriander powder
1 tsp. cumin (jeera seeds)
salt to taste
½ cup water
1.5 tsp. crushed kasuri methi (dried fenugreek leaves) (optional)
2 tbs. cilantro chopped
Juice of ½ lemon

For Rice:

1 cup basmati rice
1.5 cups water
a pinch salt (optional)

Directions

- Soak 10-12 cashews in hot water for 10 to 15 mins. Then puree in a blender to a smooth paste along with ¼ cup water. Keep it aside.
- In a blender, add diced onions, tomatoes, ginger, garlic and green chili and blend without adding water to make a smooth puree. Set it aside.
- Press SAUTE mode on Instant Pot. Add oil in to the POT.Once hot, cumin (jeera) seeds and let them splutter. Next add the pureed onion-tomato mixture, cook for around 3-4 mins until raw smell disappears.
- Then add all the dry spices coriander powder, garam masala, turmeric ,red chili powder and salt. Stir to combine.Scrape the bottom and deglaze the pot. This is an important step, to make sure you don't get the burn notice when you pressure cook.
- Add in the sliced mushrooms, peas and water. Combine gently with the masala.
- Place the trivet and then the bowl of rice with water.
- This way they will both cook together. Big advantage of the Instant Pot is the option to do Pot-in-Pot Cooking or PIP. This means you can cook multiple things at same time.
- Close the lid on the pot, and turn pressure valve to SEALING position. Set the pot to MANUAL/PRESSURE COOK (High Pressure) and set timer to 3 MINS.
- When the instant pot beeps, Let the pressure release naturally for 5 mins and then do a quick pressure release. Open the lid.
- Add cashew cream, crushed kasuri methi, coriander leaves, lemon juice and Mix well.Simmer the curry for 2 to 3 mins, the curry will thicken.

- Serve with Naan, chapatis, roti or hot basmati rice.

Mixed Veg khichdi on the Jar| Easy Lentil Rice Soup with Veggies
An Easy Weekday Dinner.

Servings: 4 Calories: 277kcal Course: Main Course Prep Time: 10 mins Cook Time: 25 mins Total Time: 30 mins

Ingredients

Jar ingredients:

3/4 cup long grain white basmati rice
3/4 cup quick cooking lentils such as Red lentils

Spices:

3/4 tsp cumin seeds
2 to 3 cloves
1 tsp coriander powder
1 tbsp onion flakes
1 tsp garlic powder
1/4 tsp ground ginger
1/2 tsp garam masala, more if you like it spicier
3/4 tsp turmeric
1/4 tsp cayenne
1 or 2 Indian bay leaves

To Cook:

1 tomato chopped
1 to 2 cups chopped vegetables
water
3/4 tsp salt

Directions

- Assemble the jar: Layer the rice and lentils.
- Toast the cumin seeds and cloves on stove top over medium heat until cumin seeds change color slightly. Cool completely.
- Add toasted cumin, cloves, rest of the spices to small ziplock bag and add to the jar. Close the lid. Store for upto 3 months.

Directions to make the khichdi On the jar:

- Wash the lentils and rice(optional).
- Add 3.5 to 4 cups water, washed lentils & rice, spice bag contents, 3/4 to 1 tsp salt and 1 tomato finely chopped.
- Add upto 2 cups of chopped vegetables and mix in. Close the lid and cook on HIGH PRESSURE for 2-4 mins. RELEASE PRESSURE after 5 mins. Fluff lightly.
- Garnish with cilantro, lemon juice and pepper flakes and serve as is or with chutneys, or papadums/crackers.

Brown Chickpea Coconut Curry | Kala Chana Curry with Coconut

Servings: 4 Calories: 252kcal Course: Main Prep Time: 10 mins Cook Time: 35 mins Total Time: 45 mins

Ingredients

Chickpeas:

3/4 cup uncooked brown chickpeas optionally soaked for 4 hours
2 cups water
1/2 cup shredded coconut fresh + more for garnish
1 tsp oil
1/2 tsp mustard seeds
6 curry leaves (optional)
a pinch of asafetida / hing optional
1/2 medium onion finely chopped
4 cloves garlic finely chopped
1 tbsp finely chopped ginger
2 tsp ground coriander
1/2 tsp ground fennel
1/4 tsp cinnamon
1/4 tsp cardamom
1/4 tsp cloves
1/3 to 1/2 tsp cayenne
1/2 tsp turmeric
2 tomatoes chopped
3/4 tsp or more salt

Tempering

1 tsp oil
1/4 tsp mustard seeds
2 dried red chilies

Directions

- Bring the brown chickpeas to a boil in 1 cup of water. Discard the water.
- Cook the chickpeas with 2 cups of water for 30 -35 mins in Instant pot (MANUAL). Let the PRESSURE RELEASE NATURALLY.
- Heat a small skillet over medium heat. Add coconut and toast for 2 to 3 mins until golden. Stir occasionally to avoid burning. Blend with 2 tbsp of water until most of the coconut breaks down and set aside.
- Heat oil in a skillet over medium heat. When hot, add mustard seeds and let them start to sputter. Add curry leaves and asafetida and cook for few seconds. They will sputter, so be careful.
- Add the onion, garlic, ginger and cook until translucent.
- Add the ground spices and mix well. for half a min. Add tomatoes and a splash of water and cook until the tomatoes are tender. 5 mins. Mash the larger pieces.
- Add this mixture, salt and the coconut paste to the brown chickpeas (or vice versa depending on the pan size) and simmer over medium heat for 5 to 10 mins. Taste and adjust salt and heat. Add more water if needed.
- Garnish with coconut.

For Tempering

- Heat oil in a small skillet over medium heat. When the oil is hot, add 1/4 tsp mustard seeds and 2 chilies and cook for a few seconds. The seeds will start to pop. Drizzle this over the chickpea curry.
- Serve over rice, cooked grains or with flatbread, appams, dosas etc.

Saag Aloo | Sweet Potato & Chard Curry
Serve this easy side with dals or curries or add to a bowl.

Servings: 3 Calories: 146kcal Course: Main Course Prep Time: 10 mins Cook Time: 20 mins Total Time: 30 mins

Ingredients

1 tsp oil
4 cloves garlic finely chopped
2 tsp minced ginger

1 small onion chopped
1 tsp ground cumin and 1/2 tsp coriander
1/2 tsp ground cinnamon
1/4 tsp ground cardamom
1/3 tsp cayenne
1 or 2 whole cloves
1/2 tsp turmeric
3/4 tsp salt
2 cups cubed sweet potato, or regular potatoes
2 cups packed chopped chard, spinach or a mix of greens
1/2 cup water
1/2 cup non dairy yogurt or full fat coconut milk
lemon and cilantro for garnish

Directions

- Heat oil in Instant pot on SAUTE. When hot, add the garlic and ginger and mix and cook for 30 seconds.
- Add the onion and pinch of salt. Mix and cook for 2 mins. Deglaze with a tbsp of water if needed, stir frequently.
- Add the spices and salt and mix in for a few seconds. Add the sweet potatoes, greens, water and yogurt and mix well to combine.
- Cancel SAUTE, close the lid and PRESSURE COOK for 4 mins (MANUAL HIGH). Then RELEASE THE PRESSURE after 5 mins
- Add some coconut milk or cashew cream for creamier if needed. Taste and adjust salt and flavor. Add some garam masala if needed. Garnish with lemon and cilantro.
- Serve with dals, beans or curries.

Khaman Dhokla | Chickpea flour Snack Cakes

Servings: 4 Calories: 249kcal Course: Breakfast Prep Time: 15 mins Cook Time: 25 mins Total Time: 40 mins

Ingredients

For the Dhokla:
2 cups chickpea flour
1 tsp salt
3/4 tsp baking soda
3/4 tsp baking powder
1/2 tsp turmeric

1/2 inch of ginger crushed or blended
1/2 green chili crushed or blended to a paste
1/2 cup non dairy yogurt plain unsweetened
1 tsp lemon juice
1/2 cup water
oil for greasing
1 Tbsp sesame seeds or shredded coconut (optional)

For the tempering:

1 tsp organic canola or safflower oil
1 tsp mustard seeds
a generous pinch of asafetida hing
1 to 2 green chili finely chopped
6 curry leaves chopped optional
1 tsp sugar
1 tsp lemon juice
1 Tbsp coconut flakes fresh or dry
½ cup water
cilantro and lemon juice for garnish

Directions

Make the Dhokla:

- Preheat the oven to 425 degrees F / 220°c. In a large bowl, add chickpeas flour, salt, baking soda, baking powder and turmeric. Whisk well.
- Add the ginger paste, chili paste, yogurt, lemon juice and mix. Add water a few Tbs. at a time to make a thick muffin type batter.
- Grease a stoneware cake pan or bread pan. sprinkle the bottom with sesame seeds or coconut shreds.
- Pour the batter into the pan, Using a greased spatula or greased hand, press or shape the batter into the pan if needed. Cover the pan with foil lightly. Prick 1-2 small holes in the center of the foil.
- Bake for 15 to 17 mins. Peak to check if the center is set. Remove from the oven and let sit for 5 mins before removing foil. Invert onto a serving dish and slice/cube.

Make the tempering:

- In a small skillet, add oil and heat at medium. When the oil is hot, add the mustard seeds and let them sizzle or sputter for a few seconds.
- Add the asafetida, chili and curry leaves. Cook for 2 to 3 mins or until most of the chili is golden brown.

- Add the sugar, lemon juice, coconut flakes and the water. Mix and cook for 3 mins or until the water is hot. Drizzle this over the dhoklas.
- Garnish with cilantro leaves and lemon juice.
- Serve with cilantro Chutney or serve as a side like cornbread. Add the tempering into the batter before baking to serve as a side.

Tikka Masala Sauce
This is a delicious freezer friendly Tikka masala sauce.

Servings: 6 Calories: 63kcal Course: Main Course Prep Time: 10 mins Cook Time: 20 mins Total Time: 30 mins

Ingredients

1 tsp oil
1 small onion chopped
6 cloves of garlic finely chopped
1 inch of ginger finely chopped
1 hot green chili
1 tsp paprika (combination of sweet and smoked)
1 tsp coriander powder
1/3 to 1/2 tsp cayenne
1/2 to 1 tsp Garam Masala
2 tsp dried fenugreek leaves, plus more for garnish
1/4 cup chopped red or green bell pepper
28 oz diced tomatoes or 15 oz diced + 2 ripe tomato chopped
1/2 cup non dairy yogurt, plain unsweetened, plain lightly sweetened also works
salt
1/4 cup non dairy cream such as cashew, soy or coconut (optional)

Directions

- Press SAUTE on Instant Pot. When hot, add the oil then add finely chopped onion, ginger, garlic, and chili. Add good pinch of salt, mix well and cook for about 3 mins. Stir occasionally
- Add the spices and mix well. Add bell pepper and mix well. Add tomatoes and non dairy yogurt and salt and mix well. (stir well for a few seconds to pick up the scorched onion bits, else they tend to scorch more and cause burn errors in some sensitive instant pots)
- Cancel SAUTE. Close the lid. PRESSURE COOK for 11-12 mins (MANUAL HIGH PRESSURE)

- Let the PRESSURE RELEASE naturally. Open the lid. mix, taste and adjust salt, flavor, heat. Add some sugar or maple syrup if needed.
- Add some more fenugreek leaves or cilantro, some fresh smoked paprika or cayenne and garam masala for garnish.
- At this point you can freeze the tikka masala sauce for upto 2 months, and refrigerate for upto 4 days.

Jeera Aloo
This is a simple yet delicious side dish.

Servings: 6 Calories: 176kcal Course: Side Dish Prep Time: 10 Mins Cook Time: 15 Mins Total Time: 25 Mins

INGREDIENTS

6 medium-sized potatoes, peeled and chopped
1 tbs. cumin seeds (jeera)
2 tbs. olive oil
½ tsp. turmeric powder
½ tsp. chili powder
1 Indian green chilies finely chopped
4 garlic cloves minced
1 tsp. salt
½ tablespoon squeezed lime juice

For garnishing

2 tbs. dried fenugreek leaves (kasoori methi)

Directions

- Add 1 cup water to the steel insert of an Instant Pot. Place a trivet and a steamer basket over it.
- Add the potatoes in the steamer basket. Cover the lid. Set the pressure to high and cook for 6 mins. Once the cooking cycle is complete, move the vent to the venting position. Remove the steamer basket carefully and set it aside.
- Add oil to a wok/kadhai kept over medium heat. When hot, add cumin seeds.
- Once the cumin seeds start to sizzle, add turmeric powder, chili powder, green chilies, and garlic cloves. Fry them for about 30 seconds.
- Add the potatoes along with salt and lime juice. Mix them well.

- Garnish with dried fenugreek leaves
- Simmer for 5 mins for the flavors to meld in. Serve hot with rotis or rice and dal.

Veg Kolhapuri | Veggies in Sesame Coconut Tomato Sauce

Servings: 4 Calories: 163kcal Course: Main Prep Time: 10 mins Cook Time: 30 mins Total Time: 40 mins

Ingredients

For the Kolhapuri Masala:

1 tsp Coriander Seeds
2 tsp Sesame seeds
1/2 tsp Poppy seeds
1/2 tsp Black pepper corns
1/2 tsp. Mustard seeds
1/4 tsp. Fenugreek seeds
1/2 tsp cumin seeds
4 dried red chilies cayenne
2 tbsp shredded coconut
1/4 tsp. Nutmeg powder
1/2 tsp or more paprika
1/4 tsp cinnamon

Sauce:

1/2 medium onion roughly chopped
2 tomatoes roughly chopped
1 inch ginger
5 cloves of garlic
1/4 tsp salt

Veggies:

2 cups cauliflower
1.5 cups sweet potato
1.5 to 2 cups other veggies carrots green beans, green peas etc
1/2 cup chopped bell pepper
1.5 to 2 cups water
Salt, cayenne to preference

Directions

- Add all ingredients coriander seeds through cumin and roast for 2 to 3 mins or until they start to change color on SAUTE mode
- Add the chilies and coconut and continue to roast for a minute or until coconut starts to change color. Take off heat and mix in the nutmeg, paprika and cinnamon. Cool slightly and grind to a coarse powder in a spice grinder or small blender.
- Add the sauce ingredients to a blender along with the ground spice mixture from above. Add a tbsp or so water and blend until smooth.
- Once the sauce is cooked, combine the sauce, chopped veggies, 1/2 to 3/4 tsp salt with 1 to 1.5 cups of water and Pressure cook for 14 to 15 mins (MANUAL) in Instant pot. Let the PRESSURE RELEASE NATURALLY, open, taste and adjust salt, garnish with cilantro and lemon.
- If there is too much liquid, cook on saute for a few mins to reduce.
- Serve

Aloo Stuffed Karela |Potato Stuffed Bitter Melon

Servings: 3 Calories: 186 kcal Course: Main course Prep Time: 15 mins Cook Time: 20 mins Total Time: 35 mins

Ingredients

7 small/medium bitter melons (karela)

Aloo Filling:

2 potatoes
1 tbs. dried mango powder amchur
1 tsp. salt
1 tsp. coriander powder
¼ tsp. black pepper
¼ tsp. cayenne
¼ tsp. roasted cumin powder
Handful cilantro leaves chopped
½ cup mustard oil

Directions

- Add 1 cup water to the steel insert in the Instant Pot and place a steamer inside the pot. Add the potatoes on top of the steamer, secure the lid, close the pressure valve and cook for 10 mins at high pressure. QUICK RELEASE and dump out the water.

- Peel some of the bumpy skin off of the bitter melons, then make a slit along the middle and spoon out any seeds. Set the melons aside for now.
- Add the cooked potatoes to a bowl along with the remaining filling ingredients and mix well.
- Spoon the filling inside the bitter melons then tie them with kitchen twine to hold the masala inside
- Pour 2 cups water into the steel insert of the Instant Pot, then place a steamer inside. Put the bitter melons in the steamer, seamed side up.
- Secure the lid, close the valve and cook for 2 mins at high pressure.
- QUICK RELEASE PRESSURE.
- Remove the melons and set them aside for now. Dump out the water from the pot and make sure to dry it completely.
- Press the SAUTÉ button, adjust the heat to its highest setting, add the mustard oil and and wait for a few mins to allow the mustard oil to get very hot (best if the screen says hot).
- Add the bitter melons to the pot with the seam side up.
- Fry the melons on all sides, turning them once they turn brown – wait to fry the stuffed side until the very end. it should take a total of 15 or so mins to get them fully browned.
- Remove the kitchen twine and serve.

Achari Paneer Biryani

Servings: 4 people Calories: 507 kcal Course: Main Course Prep Time: 10 mins Cook Time: 20 mins Total Time: 30 mins

Ingredients

2 tbs. avocado oil or olive oil
2 tsp. Indian five-spice blend - fennel, cumin, fenugreek, nigella, mustard
1 bay leaf
1 tablespoon minced ginger
1 tbs. minced garlic 3 cloves
2 serrano chilies stem removed
½ cup pureed tomato
1 cup sliced onion 1 medium
1 cup sliced bell pepper
1 tsp. red wine vinegar or juice of ½ a lime
½-1 tsp. Indian pickle (mango/mixed/chili) just the sauce, (optional)

1 cup basmati rice or any long grain rice - rinsed & soaked for 15 mins
10-12 oz paneer cut in ¾-inch cubes
1¼ cups water
2 tbs. fresh chopped cilantro for garnish

Spices

1½ tsp. salt
1 tsp. turmeric powder
1 tsp. red chili powder or paprika
1 tablespoon coriander powder
1 tsp. cumin powder
2 tsp.s garam masala
1 tsp. chaat masala

Directions

- Turn on SAUTE mode. Wait for 30-40 seconds for it to get hot. Add oil, panch puran seeds and bay leaf. Sauté for 30 seconds, until the seeds begin to sizzle.
- Add ginger, garlic and serrano chilies and SAUTÉ for another 30 seconds.
- Add tomatoes, followed by salt, turmeric, chili powder, coriander, cumin, garam masala, chaat masala, and stir. Saute for another minute. If the spices begin to stick, add a couple of tbs. of water and stir.
- Add onion, bell pepper and vinegar. Stir and sauté for 1 minute.
- Add cilantro, pickle (if using), paneer, drained rice and water, and stir well to scrape off any brown bits stuck at the bottom. Close the lid and pressure cook on High for 6 mins (sealing mode).
- When the cooking time is done, carefully RELEASE PRESSURE MANUALLY by moving the pressure knob to 'venting' in Duo models, or pushing it down in Ultra models.
- Open the lid after the pin drops. Let the biryani sit uncovered for 5 mins. After that, use a fork to fluff up the biryani.
- Garnish with the reserved cilantro and serve with pickled onions and raita.

Matar Pulao

Servings: 4 Calories: 282 kcal Course: Main course Prep Time: 30 mins Cook Time: 15 mins Total Time: 45 mins

Ingredients

1 cup basmati rice
3 tbs. oil of choice
1 tsp. cumin seeds
3 green cardamom pods
2 whole cloves
1 bay leaf
½ cinnamon stick
½ onion diced
1 cup fresh or frozen green peas
1 cup water
½ tsp. salt

Directions

- Soak the basmati rice in cold water for 15-30 mins. Drain, rinse and set aside.
- Press the SAUTE´ button, add the oil and allow it to heat up for a minute.
- Add the cumin seeds and once they begin to brown, add the cardamom, cloves, bay leaf and cinnamon stick. Give everything a quick stir, then add the diced onion.
- Stir-fry for 6-7 mins, or until the onion begins to brown. Then add the rice, peas, water and salt. Mix well.
- Secure the lid, close the pressure valve and cook for 6 mins at high pressure.
- NATURALLY RELEASE PRESSURE for 10 mins. Open the valve to release any remaining pressure.
- Fluff the rice with a fork and serve.

Easy Vegetable Korma

Servings: 4 Calories: 248 kcal Course: Curry Prep Time: 15 mins Cook Time: 20 mins Total Time: 35 mins

Ingredients

Onion Cashew Paste

1 medium sweet onion, roughly chopped
15 raw cashews
1 inch ginger
4 large garlic cloves

Vegetable Korma

2 tbs. oil 30 ml, use oil of choice
6-7 black whole peppercorns
4 green cardamoms
4 whole cloves
1 bay leaf
1/2 cup tomato puree
2 tsp.s coriander powder
1 tsp. garam masala
1/4 tsp. red chili powder or adjust to taste
1/2 tsp. turmeric powder
1/2-3/4 tsp. salt adjust to taste
1/2 cup water
1 cup coconut milk
1/2 tsp. sugar
1 large potato, cut into 1-inch pieces
1 cup large cauliflower florets
2 medium carrots 110 grams, cut into rounds
1/4 cup frozen green peas soaked in warm water for 5 mins
A pinch cardamom powder
juice of half lemon
2 tbs. chopped cilantro to garnish

Directions

- To a blender add onions, cashews, ginger and garlic. Grind to a fine paste and set aside.
- Press the SAUTE button on your Instant Pot, once it displays hot add oil to the pot and then add peppercorns, green cardamoms, whole cloves and bay leaf. Saute for few seconds until the spices are fragrant.
- Then stir in the prepared onion cashew paste and cook it for 3 to 4 mins, stirring continuously. Stirring is important else the paste will get stuck to the bottom of the pot.
- Add the tomato puree, mix and cook for another 2 mins.
- Then add in the spices - coriander powder, garam masala, red chili powder, turmeric powder and salt. Stir to combine and then add 1/2 cup of water.
- Add in the coconut milk, sugar and mix well and deglaze the pot by scrapping the bottom with a spatula. There should be nothing stuck at the bottom of the pot.
- Now add the diced potatoes and mix. Cover the pot with a glass lid and let the potatoes cook for 3 mins. The Rest of the veggies don't take much time to cook but potatoes do so this extra cooking time helps in getting the right texture for all the veggies.

- After 3 mins add in the remaining veggies - cauliflower, carrots and green peas. Add addition 1/4 cup-1/2 cup water if your Instant Pot gives BURN message.
- Stir, sprinkle cardamom powder on top and then close the instant pot with its lid. Cook on low pressure for 3 mins with the pressure valve in the SEALING position.
- Do a QUICK PRESSURE RELEASE. Open the pot, stir the veggies and then add lemon juice and cilantro.
- Serve with naan or rice!

Easy Aloo Baingan Masala | Indian Potatoes and Eggplant

Servings: 4 Calories: 175 kcal Course: Main course Prep Time: 5 mins Cook Time: 5 mins Total Time: 10 mins

Ingredients

1 tbs. oil
½ tsp. cumin seeds
½ - 1 serrano pepper minced
2-3 medium potatoes, chopped into 1-inch pieces
1 medium eggplant, chopped
¼ cup water
½ cup frozen or fresh/thawed onion masala
1 tsp. salt
½ tsp. garam masala
Cilantro to garnish

Directions

- Press the SAUTE´ button then add the oil and allow it a minute to heat up. Once the oil is hot, add the cumin seeds and serrano pepper to the pot. When the cumin seeds turn brown, add the remaining ingredients.
- Secure lid, close the pressure valve and cook for 4 mins at high pressure.
- Open the valve to quick release any remaining pressure.
- Mix well, garnish with cilantro and serve.

Garlic Naan

Servings: 12 Naan Calories: 195 kcal Course: bread, Side Dish Prep Time: 10 mins Cook Time: 10 mins Proofing: 1 hr Total Time: 1 hr 20 mins

Ingredients

¼ cup warm water microwave for 15-20 seconds
2¼ tsp.s active dry yeast 1 pack
1 tbs. sugar (added in two steps)
3 cups all-purpose flour
1½ tsp.s salt
½ cup plain Greek yogurt
¾ cup warm milk microwave for 30-40 seconds
2 tbs. olive oil and 1 tbs. for kneading

For Garlic Topping

4 tbs. butter
3-4 garlic cloves finely chopped
3-4 tbs. chopped cilantro
1 tsp. nigella seeds (kalongi)

Directions

- Microwave ¼ cup water in a cup for 15-20 seconds. The water should feel warm to the touch, not hot. Using a spoon, stir in yeast along with sugar and mix well.
- Leave aside while you assemble the other ingredients. The yeast will double in size and turn frothy.
- In the mixing bowl of a stand mixer, add flour, salt, proofed yeast, Greek yogurt, ¾ cup warm milk and 2 tbs. olive oil. Using the dough hook attachment set at low speed, mix till the ingredients to form a soft dough.
- Knead for 5 mins. Add more milk if needed, a tbs. at a time, until the dough forms into a ball.
- Add the remaining 1 tbs. olive oil and knead the dough for another 2 mins. The dough should be sticky at this point.
- Dust your hands lightly with flour, release the dough from bowl and knead into a ball.
- Grease the steel insert of the Instant Pot. Add the dough ball in the center. Cover with a glass lid and select yogurt mode, normal temperature for 1 hour.
- Grease a large mixing bowl and place the dough ball in the center. Cover the bowl with plastic wrap and let sit in a warm place for 1 hour, until doubled in size.
- Once the dough has doubled in size, turn off the yogurt mode (if using). Punch the dough 3-4 times to release some air.

- Dust your hands with flour and transfer the dough onto a rolling surface. To make even size dough balls, use a bench scraper or a chef's knife, and divide the dough into half, then quarters.
- Divide each quarter into 2 or 3 portions depending on the size of naan you prefer. Roll each dough ball to make a smooth ball.
- Using a rolling pin, roll each dough ball into a large oval shape, about 8-inches long and ¼-inch thick, using as little flour as possible. Repeat with the remaining dough.
- In a microwave safe bowl, add butter and minced garlic. Microwave for 30-40 seconds until the butter melts. Using a pastry brush, spread the garlic butter on to the rolled naan. Sprinkle some chopped cilantro and kalongi (nigella seeds). Gently press down the toppings with your hands, or roll once with the pin.
- Heat a non-stick skillet on medium-high. When hot, using a pastry brush, spread some water in the pan. Place the naan, topping side up, and let cook till large bubbles start to form (about 1- 1½ mins).
- Flip the naan and cook on the other side for another 1- 1½ mins. Remove naan to a plate and brush with some more melted garlic butter.
- Enjoy warm with your favorite Indian curry!

Paneer Butter Masala
This dish is so delicious and very easy to make.

Servings: 4 Calories: 302kcal Course: Main Course Prep Time: 5 mins Cook Time: 25 mins Total Time: 30 mins

Ingredients

1 lb Paneer or Cottage cheese chunks
2 tbsp Butter
1 Green chili pepper (optional)
1 tsp Cumin seeds (Jeera)
1 Onion cut in large pieces
1 tbsp Ginger minced
1 tbsp Garlic minced
4 Tomato cut in large pieces
¼ cup Cashews
2 tbsp Dried Fenugreek leaves
¼ cup Water
¼ cup Cream heavy whipping or coconut cream
1 tbsp Honey
1 tsp Salt adjust to taste

Spices

½ tsp Ground Turmeric
1 tsp Coriander powder
½ tsp Ground Cumin (Jeera powder) or Garam Masala
1 tsp Cayenne or Red Chili powder adjust to taste

Whole Spices

2 sticks Cinnamon
5 Green Cardamom
2 Black Cardamom
1 tsp Black Peppercorns
1 tsp Cloves

Directions

- Make a spice pouch by adding the whole spices to a cheesecloth. Tie it such that the spices cannot come out of it.
- Except paneer, cream and honey, add all ingredients and spice pouch to the Instant Pot including the spices. Close lid with vent in SEALING position.
- Set the instant pot to MANUAL or pressure cook mode on HIGH PRESSURE for 8 mins.
- After the instant pot beeps, RELEASE PRESSURE NATURALLY.
- Remove the spice pouch carefully. Blend the contents in the instant pot with an immersion blender or regular blender to a smooth paste. If using regular blender, you may need to cool the ingredients before blending. Get the contents back to the instant pot.
- Add the cream and honey. Stir into the sauce.
- Add paneer chunks. Stir them into the sauce and let it rest for 5 mins. You can cover with a glass lid.
- Paneer Butter Masala is ready to be served.
- Garnish with dry fenugreek leaves or cilantro.

Dum Aloo
Yummy Baby potatoes cooked in smooth, creamy and mouth watering sauce

Servings: 3 Calories: 315kcal Course: Entree Prep Time: 10 mins Cook Time: 20 mins
Total Time: 30 mins

Ingredients

10 baby potatoes peeled and cored
2 tbs. ghee
1 large yellow onion finely diced
2 tsp. ginger grated
2 tsp. garlic grated
2 tomatoes pureed
½ tsp. ground turmeric
1 tablespoon red chili powder
½ tsp. garam masala
1 tsp. kosher salt
15 cashews
¼ cup warm milk or water for dairy free
1 tablespoon dried fenugreek leaves
¼ cup cilantro chopped for garnish

Directions

- Soak cashews in warm milk for 10 mins and set aside. Blend together to make smooth paste and reserve.
- Set the Instant Pot to SAUTE mode and heat add ghee. Add onions and cook for 2 mins with a glass lid on, stirring few times. Add ginger and garlic paste, cook for 30 seconds.
- Add the carved out pieces from the potatoes. Add tomato puree, turmeric, red chili powder, garam masala and salt. Cook everything on SAUTE mode for 2 mins with glass lid on, stirring a couple of times.
- With a small spoon, very carefully, as the gravy will be hot, fill the potatoes with the cooked masala/gravy and line them all in the IP insert. Add ½ cup of water. Close the Instant Pot, and PRESSURE COOK(Hi) for 8 mins followed by QUICK RELEASE.
- Stir in dried fenugreek leaves, cashew paste and chopped cilantro. Set the Instant Pot to SAUTÉ mode and mix everything together. Add salt to taste. Bring to gentle boil and then turn the Instant Pot off.
- Serve with hot parathas.

Chana Saag | Chickpea Spinach Curry

Servings: 4 Calories: 209kcal Course: Entrée Prep Time: 10 mins Cook Time: 40 mins Total Time: 50 mins

Ingredients

3/4 cup dried chickpeas soaked for atleast 4 hours in warm water
1 tsp oil
1/2 medium onion finely chopped
1 hot green chile finely chopped
4-5 cloves of garlic minced
1 inch ginger peeled and minced
1/2 tsp each ground cumin garam masala, paprika
1 tsp ground coriander
15 oz can tomatoes or 2 large tomatoes diced
1.5 cups water
3/4 tsp or more salt
2-3 packed cups chopped spinach
1 cup non dairy milk
1 tbsp or more lemon juice
cayenne and garam masala for garnish

Directions

- Drain the soaked chickpeaas, wash well, drain and set aside.
- Press SAUTE on the Instant pot. Let the pot get hot for 2 mins. Add oil and spread using a spatula.
- Meanwhile. Mince and mix together or process the onion, ginger, garlic and hot chile. Add to the hot oil. Cook for 3 to 4 mins, stirring frequently.
- Add the spices (cumin garam masala, paprika, coriander) and mix in. Add the tomatoes and bring to a boil. Mash the larger pieces.
- Add washed and drained chickpeas, salt and water. Close the lid and put the knob on sealing.
- PRESSURE COOK for 25 to 30 mins. QUICK RELEASE after 10 mins. Press saute. Fold in the greens and non dairy mil.. Taste and adjust salt.
- Cook for 2 to 4 mins to wilt the greens.
- Add cayenne and lemon juice and mix in. Serve hot over rice or with roti or naan.

Sukha Kala Chana | Dry Black Chickpeas

This is a flavorful easy side dish on busy weeknights.

Servings: 8 Calories: 142kcal Course: Side Dish Prep Time: 5 Mins Cook Time: 25 Mins Total Time: 50 Mins

Ingredients

1.5 cups black chickpeas / chana
1 tsp. salt
1 tablespoon oil or ghee
1 tsp. cumin seeds
½ tsp. turmeric powder
½ tsp. chili powder optional
2 Indian or Thai green chilies slit lengthwise
2 tsp.s coriander powder
½ tsp. amchur powder
½ tsp. garam masala powder
salt to taste

Directions

- Rinse and soak the chickpeas in 3 cups of water overnight or at least for 6-8 hours
- Drain the chickpeas and add them to Instant Pot along with 2 cups of water
- Cook the chickpeas in the Instant Pot, select 'Pressure Cook' and set the timer for 25 mins. When the cooking cycle is complete, allow the pressure to RELEASE NATURALLY.
- Drain the chickpeas and reserve the liquid to use it in roti dough or dals.
- Heat the oil in a medium-sized pan over medium heat and add cumin seeds to it.
- When the cumin seeds start to sizzle, add all the spice powders – coriander, turmeric, chili, turmeric along with green chilies (if using) and SAUTE it for about 10-20 seconds making sure it doesn't burn.
- Add the drained chickpeas and mix well.
- Do a taste test and add more salt if needed.
- Simmer it for 5 mins and take it off heat.
- Serve hot with poori and halwa or enjoy it a side dish with dal and rice.

Cabbage Potato Peas Curry

A delicious curry made with cabbage, potatoes, green peas that's infused with Indian spices and extremely easy to make.

Servings: 4 Calories: 245kcal Course: Side Dish Prep Time: 10 mins Cook Time: 10 mins Total Time: 20 mins

Ingredients

4 cups cabbage shredded
2 medium potato diced into 1 inch pieces
½ fresh/frozen cup green peas
1 tbs. coconut oil
½ tsp. cumin seeds (jeera)
2 green chilies finely chopped
1 tbs. ginger garlic paste
1 medium onion finely chopped
½ cup water + 2 tbs. extra water
1 tbs. lemon juice or amchur powder
2 tbs. chopped cilantro/coriander leaves (optional)
salt to taste

Dry Spices:

½ tsp. ground turmeric (haldi)
½ tsp. red chilli powder or cayenne pepper (lal mirch)
1 tsp. coriander powder
1 tsp. garam masala

Directions

- Press SAUTE mode on Instant Pot. Add oil, Once hot, add cumin seeds, let them splutter. Next add ginger garlic paste, green chilies and onions and saute till onions turn soft.
- Add diced potatoes and cook for 2-3 mins till they are semi cooked
- Next add spices like turmeric powder, coriander powder, red chilli powder, garam masala ,salt ,remaining water and mix well. Make sure to scrap of any spice if sticking to the pot to avoid BURN alert.
- Next add the shredded cabbage, peas, mix well. Add extra 2 tbs. of water at this stage if you want. Close the lid on the pot, and turn pressure valve to SEALING position.

- Set the pot to MANUAL/PRESSURE COOK (High Pressure) and set timer to 1 minute. When the instant pot beeps, Do a QUICK RELEASE.
- Remove lid away from you, sprinkle coriander leaves and lemon juice, Mix well.
- Serve with hot with chapatis, roti & parathas.

Sambar | Split Pigeon Pea and Vegetable Soup

Servings: 4 Calories: 305 kcal Course: Main course Prep Time: 1 hr Cook Time: 10 mins Total Time: 1 hr 10 mins

Ingredients

1 cup split pigeon peas (toor dal)
1 tbs. oil of choice
½ tsp. black mustard seeds
¼ tsp. fenugreek seeds
15 curry leaves
1 tsp. minced garlic
1 tsp. minced ginger

Spices

2 tsp. coriander powder
2 tsp. salt
1 tsp. paprika
½ tsp. turmeric
¼ tsp. black pepper
¼ tsp. cayenne
¼ tsp. roasted cumin powder
⅛ tsp. hing (optional)
4 cups water
3 cups chopped mixed vegetables
1 tomato chopped
½ onion chopped into chunks
1 tsp. sugar
1 tsp. tamarind paste

Directions

- Soak the split pigeon peas (toor dal) in cold water for 1 hour. Drain, rinse and set aside.

- Press the SAUTE´ button, add the oil and allow it to heat up for a minute. Add the mustard seeds and fenugreek seeds.
- Once the mustard seeds begin to splutter, add the curry leaves, garlic, ginger and spices. Stir, then add the remaining ingredients and mix well.
- Secure the lid, close the pressure valve and cook for 10 mins at high pressure.
- NATURALLY RELEASE PRESSURE for 15 mins. Open the valve to release any remaining pressure.
- Serve over rice or with idli or dosa.

Dal Palak | Spinach Dal
This is a delicious lentil dish with added spinach. Enjoy with rice or as a soup.

 Servings: 4 Calories: 153kcal Course: Main Course Prep Time: 10 mins Cook Time: 15 mins Total Time: 25 mins

Ingredients

1 cup Split Pigeon Pea (Toor dal) washed
2 cup Spinach (Palak) chopped
1 tbs. Ghee or Oil
½ tsp. Cumin seeds (Jeera)
1 Green Chili Pepper sliced (optional)
½ Ginger finely chopped
4 cloves Garlic finely chopped
1 Tomato large, chopped
3 cups Water
½ tsp. Garam Masala

Spices

1 tsp. Salt
¼ tsp. Ground Turmeric (Haldi powder)
¼ tsp. Cayenne or Red Chili powder

Directions

- Start the instant pot in SAUTE mode and heat oil in it. Add cumin seeds, green chili, ginger and garlic.
- Saute for 30 seconds until garlic turns golden brown, then add chopped tomato and spices.

- Add the lentils and water. Stir well. Press CANCEL and close the instant pot lid with vent in sealing position.
- Press MANUAL or Pressure Cook mode for 3 mins. When the instant pot beeps, do a quick pressure release.
- Open the lid and add chopped spinach and garam masala. Press SAUTE mode. Simmer for 2 mins until the dal starts boiling and spinach is mixed with the lentils.
- Spinach dal is ready to be served.

Sooji Halwa - Rava Sheera| Spoon Fudge

Servings: 4 Calories: 479kcal Course: Dessert Prep Time: 10 mins Cook Time: 15 mins Total Time: 25 mins

Ingredients

3 tbsp vegan butter or oil
1 cup sooji (semolina, not semolina flour)
5 tbsp cashews
10 to 12 dates chopped
8 to 10 tbsp sugar
1/8 tsp salt
3/4 tsp ground cardamom
8 strands of saffron
3 cups water

Directions

- Press SAUTE on the Instant Pot. When hot, add vegan butter or oil. Add cashews and roast for a minute.
- Add dates and roast for half a minute. Add the semolina and cook for 2 mins, stirring occasionally. The semolina will start to get puffy.
- Switch off SAUTE. Add the sugar, salt, cardamom and saffron and mix.
- Add water and mix well. You can also add 1/2 cup finely chopped pineapple or banana at this point to make pineapple kesari or banana kesari.
- Mix to pick up all the semolina from the bottom and the sides. Mix for a few seconds so the sugar dissolves.
- Close the lid, PRESSURE COOK for 3 mins. RELEASE PRESSURE after 10 mins
- Mix and Fluff and serve garnished with a pinch of ground cardamom and almond, pistachio slivers.

Dal Makhani

A rich creamy, rich and flavor packed lentil curry with aromatics and toasted spices.

Servings: 4 Calories: 229 kcal Course: Main Course Prep Time: 8 hrs 10 mins Cook Time: 45 mins Total Time:8 hrs 55 mins

Ingredients

Wash & Soak

½ cup black gram (Whole Urad) 8 hours in 3 cups water/overnight
¼ cup red kidney beans (Rajma) 8 hours in 3 cups water/ overnight

Curry

1 tablespoon butter or olive oil
1 tsp. cumin seeds
1 cup chopped onion about 1 medium onion
1-2 green chillies tops chopped
1 tablespoon ginger paste
3 cloves garlic minced or finely chopped
1 cup pureed tomatoes 2 medium roma tomatoes pureed

Spices

¾ tsp. salt adjust to taste
¼ tsp. turmeric powder
2 tsp. garam masala
2 tsp. ground coriander
1 tsp. kashmiri red chili powder
2 cups water

Add after Pressure cooking

¼ tsp. garam masala
1 tsp. butter (optional)
2 tbs. heavy whipping cream
2 tablespoon chopped cilantro

Directions

- Soak 8 hrs (or overnight)
- Wash and soak black gram and red kidney beans in water for 8 hours to overnight. Later, strain and rinse the lentils well. Keep aside.

Pressure Cook

- Turn on SAUTE mode. Add butter (or oil) and let it heat up. Add cumin seeds and wait for them to sizzle.
- Add onions and SAUTE for 3 mins, until translucent. Add ginger and garlic paste and SAUTE another minute. Now add pureed tomato and deglaze the pot, which means scrap off any brown bits at the bottom of the pot.
- Add salt, turmeric, garam masala, coriander, red chili powder, followed by strained lentils and water.
- Close the lid and set vent to SEALING position. PRESSURE COOK for 30 mins on Bean/Chili or MANUAL mode, at HIGH PRESSURE. After the cook time is over, let the PRESSURE RELEASE NATURALLY. Open the lid after the pin drops.

After Pressure Cooking

- Using a potato masher, mash a few times to make it naturally creamy. Sprinkle ¼ tsp. garam masala, add heavy cream, butter, and let it simmer on saute mode for 3-5 mins. Garnish with cilantro and serve!

Eggplant Sambar| Yellow Lentil Tamarind Dal

Servings: 4 Calories: 211kcal Course: dal, Main Prep Time: 10 mins Cook Time: 30 mins Total Time: 40 mins

Ingredients

1 tsp. safflower or other neutral oil
1/2 tsp. black mustard seeds
1/4 tsp fenugreek seeds (optional)
2 dried red chilies (optional)
10 curry leaves coarsely chopped
3 cloves garlic chopped
1/2 cup chopped red onion or sliced pearl onions
1 tsp sambhar powder
2 medium tomatoes chopped
1/2 tsp. ground turmeric
1 to 2 cup chopped eggplant
1/2 cup chopped green bell pepper or 1/2 cup chopped carrots
1 tsp salt

1 cup split peas, washed, soaked for 15 mins and drained
2.5 cups to 4 cups water
1 to 2 tsp. tamarind paste concentrate
cilantro and lemon for garnish

Directions

- Heat the oil in the Instant Pot on SAUTE. When the oil is hot, add the mustard seeds, and cook until they start to pop, about 10 seconds.
- Add the fenugreek seeds, red chiles, and curry leaves carefully, and cook for a few seconds. Add the garlic and onion and cook until translucent, about 5 mins
- Add the sambhar powder, mix, and cook for half a minute. Add tomatoes, turmeric, and mix. Cook until the tomatoes are saucy, 6 to 8 mins. Add the vegetables and mix in.
- Add the drained split peas, salt, tamarind and water. Mix, close the lid and cook for 10 to 15 mins. Let the PRESSURE RELEASE NATURALLY.
- Add more tamarind extract if needed. Taste and adjust salt and heat.
- Add a pinch of sugar to balance the tang if needed.
- Garnish with cilantro and lemon juice.
- Serve as a soup or over rice or with dosa crepes or steamed rice cakes.

Brown Rice Lobia Pulao| Black Eyed Peas Pulao

Servings: 4 Calories: 274kcal Course: Main Course Prep Time: 10 mins Cook Time: 30 mins Total Time: 40 mins

Ingredients

1/2 cup uncooked/dry black eyed peas
2/3 cup brown basmati rice
1 tsp oil
1/3 tsp cumin seeds
1/3 tsp mustard seeds
3 cloves
1/4 cup raw or roasted peanuts, or use cashews
1/2 onion chopped
5 cloves of garlic chopped
1/2 inch ginger chopped
1/2 hot green chile optional
1/2 tsp turmeric
1 tsp coriander powder
1/2 to 1 tsp garam masala or 1 to 1.5 tsp biryani masala

1/3 tsp cayenne less or more to preference
1 large tomato chopped
1/2 bell pepper chopped, or other veggies
1 3/4 cup water
3/4 to 1 tsp salt
lemon juice, cilantro for garnish

Directions

- Soak the black eyed peas and basmati rice in hot water for 20-30 mins. In the meanwhile, prep and follow the next steps.
- Press SAUTE mode on IP. Add oil and let it get hot. Add the seeds and cloves and cook for half a minute. Add the nuts and cook for a minute to roast. Add the onion, ginger, garlic, and chile and a pinch of salt and cook for 2 mins. Stir occasionally.
- Add the ground spices (turmeric through cayenne) and mix in. Add the tomato and peppers and mix in. Cook for a minute.
- Drain the black eyed peas and rice and add to the pot. Add water and salt and mix in.
- PRESSURE COOK for 18 to 20 mins. Let the PRESSURE RELEASE naturally.
- Taste and adjust salt. Add more garam masala or other spices if needed and mix in.
- Add a good dash of lemon and cilantro, some chopped red onion and serve with pappadum or crackers.

Butter Chickpeas |Vegan Butter Chicken

Servings: 4 Calories: 250 kcal Course: main course Prep Time: 10 mins Cook Time: 35 mins Total Time: 45 mins

Ingredients

2 cups dried chickpeas soaked overnight
2 tbs. oil of choice
1 onion diced
3 tsp. minced garlic
1 tsp. minced ginger

Spices

1 ½ tsp.s garam masala
1 tsp. coriander powder

1 tsp. paprika
1 tsp. salt
1 tsp. turmeric
¼ tsp. black pepper
¼ tsp. cayenne adjust to taste
¼ tsp. ground cumin
1 15 ounce can tomato sauce
1 ½ cups water

Other ingredients:

1 green bell pepper chopped into large pieces
½ cup unsweetened cream
Pinch of dried fenugreek leaves kasoori methi
Cilantro to garnish

Directions

- Soak the chickpeas in cold water overnight. Drain, rinse and set aside.
- Press the SAUTE´ button. Add the oil and allow it to heat it up for a minute. Add the onion and stir-fry for 6-7 mins, or until the onion begins to brown.
- Add the garlic, ginger and spices stir, then add the chickpeas, tomato sauce and water.
- Secure the lid, close the pressure valve and cook for 35 mins at high pressure.
- NATURALLY RELEASE PRESSURE.
- Add the bell pepper, cream and fenugreek leaves to the pot and mix well.
- Garnish with cilantro and serve.

Chicken Saag - Soy Curls in Spinach Sauce.

Servings: 3 Calories: 184kcal Course: Main Course Prep Time: 10 mins Cook Time: 25 mins Total Time: 35 mins

Ingredients

1 small onion
5 cloves of garlic
1/2 inch ginger
1/2 hot green chile
3/4 cup tomato
4 to 5 oz spinach or spinach + other greens such as baby kale
1 cinnamon stick, 2 inch long

2 cloves
1 or 2 bay leaves
1/2 tsp turmeric
1/2 tsp garam masala
1/2 tsp coriander powder
1/2 tsp paprika
1.5 cups soy curls, dry
3/4 tsp salt
1/4 cup cashew cream or 1/3 cup vegan plain yogurt
1/2 to 1 tsp sugar or sweetener
cayenne and garam masala to taste
1 tsp fenugreek leaves (optional)

Directions

- Blend the onion through tomato and set aside. Blend the spinach/greens with 1/4 cup water. Pulse to make a coarse mixture and not a puree.
- Heat oil in SAUTE mode. When hot, add cinnamon, cloves and bay leaf. Cook for a few seconds.
- Add blended onion tomato mix. Cook for 3 mins, stir frequently. If it starts to burn, switch off saute for 2 mins, then switch on again if needed. Add the spices and mix in.
- Add the greens, soy curls and salt. Add 1/2 cup water and mix in.
- Cook on MANUAL/PRESSURE COOK (hi) 8 to 10 mins. Release after 5 mins.
- Fold in cashew cream or yogurt and mix in. Add some water if needed and cook on saute until the mixture starts to boil. Add cayenne, garam masala, sugar and mix in. Adjust salt, spice and heat. Add fenugreek leaves if using.
- Serve garnished with pepper flakes with rice, quinoa or with flatbread or pita bread.

Potato Curry | Aloo Rasedar
Easy and delicious Potato Curry in Tomato Gravy.

Servings: 3 Calories: 224kcal Course: Main Course Prep Time: 5 mins CookTime: 15 mins Total Time: 20 mins

Ingredients

2 tbsp Oil
1 tsp Cumin seeds (Jeera)
¼ tsp Asafoetida (Hing) optional

1 tbsp Ginger minced
1 cup Tomato chopped
3 Potatoes cut into small cubes about ½ inch
1 cup Water

Spices

2 tsp Coriander powder (Dhaniya powder)
¼ tsp Ground Turmeric (Haldi powder)
½ tsp Cayenne or Red Chili powder adjust to taste
½ tsp Salt adjust to taste

To finish

½ tsp Garam masala adjust to taste
1 tsp Dry Mango powder (Amchur) or 1 tbsp lime juice
Cilantro to garnish

Directions

- Start the Instant pot in SAUTE mode and let it heat. Add oil, cumin seeds, asafoetida and ginger. Saute for 30 seconds.
- Add tomatoes and spices. Saute for 3 mins. Add potatoes and water. Stir well. Press CANCEL and close lid with vent in SEALING position.
- Start on MANUAL/PRESSURE Cook mode at HIGH PRESSURE for 2 mins. When the pressure cooker beeps, press cancel and QUICK RELEASE the PRESSURE MANUALLY.
- Add garam masala and dry mango powder. Stir and mash some potatoes with the back of the ladle. This will help thicken the curry. If you like a thinner gravy, you can add some water and let it come to a boil on sauté mode.
- Garnish with cilantro and enjoy with poori, naan or rice.

Baingan Bharta Recipe|Spiced Mashed Eggplant
1 Pot dish that can serve as dip with flatbread, curries or Dals.

Servings: 4 Calories: 55kcal Course: Main Cuisine Prep Time:5 mins Cook Time:20 mins Total Time: 25 mins

Ingredients

2 tsp oil

1/2 tsp cumin seeds
3/4 cup onion chopped
1 inch ginger finely chopped
5 cloves of garlic finely chopped
1 hot green chilli finely chopped
1 tsp turmeric
1/2 tsp garam masala
1 tsp ground coriander
1/2 tsp smoked paprika
1 large tomato (diced)
1 large eggplant peeled and cubed
Salt to taste
1/2 cup water
1/3 cup peas
1/4 cup cilantro

Directions

- Set your instant pot to SAUTÉ, once it has heated up, add oil. Let the oil heat up and add the cumin seeds. COOK for half a minute. Add the onion, ginger, garlic, green chili and a good pinch of salt. Cook for 3 mins.
- Add all the ground spices and mix well. Then add the tomato and allow to cook for 2 mins. Mash the larger pieces of tomato and deglaze with a tbsp of water if needed.
- Once the tomato is tender, add the eggplant, salt, water and give it a good mix. Cancel SAUTÉ mode, close the lid, then pressure cook for 9-10 mins. Let the pressure release naturally.
- Open the lid and mash the eggplants really well using a potato masher. Taste and adjust the salt and flavor as needed. Add 1/2 tsp. of liquid smoke for additional smoky flavor. Press SAUTÉ mode and cook for 3 mins, stirring occasionally, (cook a few mins longer for thicker and more roasted) then add the peas and cilantro and mix in. Cancel SAUTÉ.
- Serve hot and garnish with additional cilantro, pepper flakes and sprinkle smoked paprika.

Madras Lentils with Brown Rice
This restaurant style dish is rich, creamy and flavorful.

Servings: 4 Calories: 251kcal Course: Main Course Prep Time: 10 mins Cook Time: 50 mins Total Time: 1 hr

Ingredients

1 cup Black gram lentils (Sabut Urad Dal) rinsed and soaked for 4 hours or overnight
¼ cup Red Kidney Beans (Rajma)
1 tbsp Butter or Oil
1 tsp Cumin seeds (Jeera)
1 tbsp Ginger minced
1 tbsp Garlic minced
Onion medium, diced
2 Tomato medium, diced
3 cup Water for cooking
1 tbsp Lemon juice (optional)
Cilantro to garnish

Spices

1 tsp red chili powder
½ tsp Garam Masala
1 tsp Coriander powder
1 tsp Salt adjust to taste

For Brown Rice

1 cup Brown Rice rinsed
1.25 cup Water
1 tbsp Ghee or Oil (optional)
1 tsp Salt

Directions

- Rinse and soak lentils and beans in water for 4 hours or overnight.
- Start the Instant pot in SAUTE mode and let it heat. Add oil and cumin seeds.
- When the cumin seeds change color, add onions, ginger and garlic. Sauté for about 3 mins.
- Add tomatoes and spices. Stir and saute for another 2 mins.
- Drain the water from the soaked lentils and beans. Add them to the instant pot. Add water and mix the ingredients.
- In a steel bowl, add the ingredients for brown rice. Please a tall trivet and the bowl of rice on top of the trivet.
- Press cancel and close the lid with vent in sealing position. Change the instant pot setting to bean/chili, which will set the timer to 30 mins of HIGH PRESSURE cooking.
- When the instant pot beeps, do a natural pressure release. Open the lid.

- (optional) Using tongs, carefully take out the bowl of basmati rice. Then take out the trivet.
- Stir the dal well. If needed, add water to get the desired consistency. If you like, add more garam masala to taste.
- Stir in the lemon juice and garnish with cilantro. It is ready to be served.

Cauliflower Coconut Curry
This recipe is delicious, healthy and easy to make.

Servings: 6 Calories: 88kcal Course: Main Course Prep Time: 10 mins Cook Time: 5 mins Total Time: 15 mins

Ingredients

1 tbs. coconut oil
1 bay leaf
1 tsp. cumin (jeera) seeds
1 large onion finely chopped
1 tablespoon ginger garlic paste
1 can tomatoes crushed (about 1.5 cups)
1 can full fat coconut milk (about 1.5 cups)
1 large head cauliflower
salt to taste
Juice of half lemon
2 tbs. cilantro/coriander leaves

Dry Spices

½ tsp. turmeric powder
1 tsp. red chilli powder
1 tsp. coriander powder
1 tsp. garam masala powder

Directions

- Press SAUTE on Instant Pot. Add coconut oil in to the POT.Once oil is hot add cumin seeds, bay leaf and let cumins splutter.
- Then add onions, ginger garlic paste and saute until onions turn light brown for 3-4 mins.

- Next add the crushed tomatoes along with the juice or tomato puree/sauce, full fat coconut milk and dry spices like red chilli powder, turmeric powder, garam masala powder, coriander powder, salt, cauliflower florets and Stir well.
- Make sure to Deglaze the bottom of the pot to remove any stuck bits.
- If you think mixture is too thick add ½ cup of water to this.
- Close the lid on the pot. Select 0 mins on MANUAL/PRESSURE COOK (High Pressure) OR select Manual 2 mins for low pressure
- Once the pot beeps, Quick release the pressure manually.
- Squeeze some fresh lemon juice and garnish with cilantro. Dont worry if the curry is too liquid consistency. Just turn on SAUTE mode again and boil the curry for 2-3 mins or until you get desired consistency.
- Serve with hot with Basmati rice, Jeera Rice or quinoa.

Punjabi Kadhi Chawal | Yogurt Curry with Rice
This is a delicious one-pot Instant pot recipe for a classic Indian food.

Servings: 6 Calories: 249 kcal Course: Main Course Prep Time: 5 mins Cook Time: 6 mins Total Time: 30 mins

Ingredients

For Kadhi

1½ cups low-fat plain yogurt, can use whole milk too
½ cup besan (chickpea flour)
¾ tsp. turmeric powder
½ tsp. cayenne
4 cups water
1 tbs. ghee or oil
1 tsp. mustard seeds
½ tsp. fenugreek seeds (Methi Seeds)
6-7 curry leaves (optional)
1-2 green chillies whole. (optional)
1 medium onion thinly sliced (1 cup)
1½ tsp. salt

Rice

1 cup basmati rice rinsed 2-3 times, soaked for 10 mins
1¼ cup water
1 tsp. oil

½ tsp. salt
Onion-Spinach Pakoras (Fritters) optional
1 cup besan (chickpea flour)
1 tsp. salt adjust to taste
½ tsp. turmeric powder
1-2 tsp. coriander
1 tsp. chaat masala
1 tsp. roasted cumin powder
½ tsp. cayenne adjust to taste
½ tsp. baking soda
½ cup water adjust for pancake batter-like consistency
1 cup baby spinach chopped
1 medium shallot chopped or sliced thin
2 tbs. light olive oil for pan-frying

Garnish

1 tsp. roasted cumin powder
2 tbs. chopped cilantro

Directions

Assembling Kadhi in Instant Pot

- Add sifted chickpeas flour (besan) to the yogurt. Add salt, turmeric, cayenne and water. Using a hand blender or a wire whisk, mix everything well to form a smooth, lump-free batter.
- Melt ghee on SAUTE mode in Instant Pot. Add mustard and fenugreek seeds. Once the seeds begin to splutter (in a few seconds), add curry leaves (optional), green chillies and sliced shallots (or onions) and saute for one minute. Add the yogurt mix and stir well.

Pot-in-Pot Rice (optional)

- If making rice in the same pot, place the trivet in the instant pot. In a smaller bowl, combine rinsed rice, salt, water and oil. Place the bowl on the trivet.

Rajma Masala|Kidney Beans Curry
This is a one-pot healthy, protein-rich recipe made with dry or canned beans and cooked in a spicy, flavorful onion-tomato gravy along with few spices

Servings: 4 Calories: 208 Course: Main Course Prep Time: 10 mins Cook Time: 40 mins Total Time: 50 mins

Ingredients

1 cup dried red kidney beans
1 large onion finely chopped
2 large tomatoes finely chopped
1 tbs. ginger garlic paste
1 tsp. cumin seeds(jeera)
1 bay leaf
½ tsp. turmeric powder
1 tsp. red chilli powder
1 tsp. coriander powder
½ tsp. garam masala
1 tbs. dried kasuri methi
2 cups water
salt to taste
cilantro/coriander leaves
1 tsp. amchur powder or lime juice
2 tablespoon oil

Directions

- Soak the kidney beans for at least 4+ hours in hot water or overnight. Drain water and keep aside.
- Press SAUTE mode on Instant Pot. Add oil in to the POT.
- Once POT is hot add cumin seeds, bay leaf, let the cumin splutter
- Next add onions, ginger garlic paste and saute until onions turn light brown for 3-4 mins.
- Next add finely chopped tomatoes or tomato puree and cook for 2-3 mins.
- Add the spices red chilli powder, turmeric powder, coriander powder, kidney beans, salt and water for cooking. Stir well.
- Close the lid on the pot, and turn pressure valve to SEALING position.
- Set the pot to "BEAN/CHILI" Mode and set timer to 30 mins.
- Do a NATURAL PRESSURE RELEASE (NPR)
- Remove lid away from you, add garam masala powder, kasuri methi, cilantro and amchur powder or lime juice. Mix well.
- Dont worry if the curry is too liquid consistency. Just turn on SAUTE mode again and boil the curry for 5 mins or until you get desired consistency.
- Serve with hot with pooris, chapatis, roti & parathas.

Aloo Palak Dal | Spiced Potato Spinach Lentils

Servings: 2 Calories: 192kcal Course: Main Course Prep Time: 10 mins Cook Time: 30 mins Soaking time: 1 hr Total Time: 40 mins

Ingredients

1/3 cup uncooked brown lentils
1 tsp oil
4 cloves of garlic minced
1 inch ginger minced
1 hot green chile chopped
2 large tomatoes chopped
1/2 tsp garam masala
1/4 tsp cinnamon
1/4 tsp cardamom
1/2 tsp turmeric
2 medium potatoes cubed
1/2 tsp salt
1 cup water
5 to 6 oz Spinach

Directions

- Soak the lentils for at least an hour else they will not cook within the time and the potatoes will get over cooked in the more time needed to cook lentils.
- In SAUTE mode, add oil, ginger, garlic, chile and cook until translucent. Add tomato and spices and cook until tomatoes are tender. Mash the larger pieces. 4 to 5 mins.
- Add the potatoes, drained lentils, water, salt and mix in. Add in the spinach or greens and mix in. Close the lid and cook on MANUAL (HIGH PRESSURE) for 7 to 8 mins. Let the PRESSURE RELEASE NATURALLY.
- Open, taste and adjust salt and spice. Add more spices or garam masala if needed.
- Garnish with cilantro, pepper flakes and lemon and serve over rice or with roti/flatbread.

Lauki Ki Sabji (Bottle Gourd Curry)

A simple and healthy curry prepared with Bottle Gourd aka Lauki, and few spices.

Servings: 4 Calories: 94kcal Course: Side Dish Prep Time : 10 mins Cook Time : 15 mins Total Time : 25 mins

Ingredients

500 grams bottle gourd peeled and chopped about ½ inch pieces
2 tbs. coconut oil
1 tsp. cumin seeds
1 stalk curry leaves
2 green chilies finely chopped
1-inch ginger finely chopped
1 medium onion finely chopped
2 small tomatoes finely chopped
¼ cup water
salt to taste
2 tbs. cilantro/coriander leaves

Dry Spices

½ tsp. turmeric powder
½ tsp. red chilli powder
1 tsp. coriander powder
1 tsp. garam masala
½ tsp. amchur powder/ 1 tbs. of lime juice

Directions

- Wash Bottle Gourd, peel the skin and cut into ½ inch pieces.
- Press SAUTE mode on Instant Pot. Add oil in to the POT.
- Once hot, add cumin seeds, let them splutter.
- Next add minced ginger, green chili and curry leaves. Saute for 30 secs.
- Add chopped onion and saute till onions turn light brown in color.
- Next add tomatoes and cook for 2 more mins till tomatoes turn soft.
- Add all the dry spices like turmeric powder, red chili powder, coriander pow-der, garam masala powder, lauki/bottle gourd pieces, water, salt and mix well.
- Deglaze the pot i.e., Make sure to scrap any spice that is sticking to the pot, to avoid BURN alert.
- Close the lid on the pot, and turn pressure valve to SEALING position. Press CANCEL button on Instant Pot.
- Set the pot to MANUAL/PRESSURE COOK (High Pressure) and set timer to 5 MINS.
- When the instant pot beeps, Do a QUICK RELEASE.
- Remove lid away from you, squeeze lemon juice and garnish with cilantro/coriander leaves and Mix well.
- Serve with hot with chapatis, roti & parathas.

Tomato Coconut Soup
A soothing, flavorful, spicy, & tasty Soup

Servings: 4 Calories: 157kcal Course: Main Courses, Soups Prep Time: 5 mins Cook Time: 20 mins Total Time: 25 mins

Ingredients

1 can Full-Fat Coconut Milk, full fat
1 Red Onion. chopped, diced
6 Tomatoes, chopped in quarters
1/4 cup Cilantro, chopped
1 tsp. Garlic, minced
1 tsp. Minced Ginger, minced
1 tsp. Kosher Salt
1/2 tsp. Cayenne Pepper
1 tsp. Turmeric
1 tbs. agave nectar

Directions

- Put all ingredients into the Instant Pot and cook on High for 5 mins. Allow the pot to sit undisturbed for 10 mins. After that, RELEASE PRESSURE. If you start to see sputtering and spewing from the valve, close the valve and try again in 5 mins.
- Remove from the pot and use an immersion blender to mix all the ingredients together and get a smooth soup.

Langar Dal

Servings: 4 Calories: 142 kcal Course: Main course Prep Time: 10 mins Cook Time: 30 mins Total Time: 40 mins

Ingredients

4 tbs. ghee
1 tsp. cumin seeds
1 cup whole black urad dal soaked in cold water overnight
¼ cup chana dal rinsed

4 cups water
1 cup frozen or thawed onion masala
1 ½ tsp. salt
1 ½ tsp. garam masala
½ tsp. cayenne

Garnish (Optional)

Cream
Cilantro leaves

Directions

- Press the SAUTÉ button, add 2 tbs. of ghee to the pot and once that melts add the cumin seeds. When the cumin seeds turn brown, add the remaining ingredients to the pot.
- Secure the lid, close the pressure valve and cook for 30 mins at high pressure.
- NATURALLY RELEASE PRESSURE.
- Stir in the remaining 2 tbs. of ghee and garnish with a drizzle of heavy cream and cilantro if desired. The dal will continue to thicken as it cools.
- If you have frozen cubes of onion masala, just toss those in – no need to thaw them first.
- This dal will thicken as it cools.

Mushroom Masala in Creamy Sauce

Servings: 3 Calories: 144kcal Course: Main Course Prep Time:10 mins Cook Time:20 mins Total Time: 30 mins

Ingredients

1/2 large onion chopped
5 cloves garlic
1 inch ginger
1/2 to 1 green chile
1 tsp oil
2 large tomatoes
1/2 to 1 tsp garam masala
1/2 tsp paprika
1/4 tsp turmeric
1 tsp dried fenugreek leaves (kasuri methi) or use 1/4 tsp fenugreek seed powder
8 oz sliced white mushrooms

1/2 tsp or more salt
1/2 cup or more peas
1 cup chopped spinach
1/4 tsp or more sugar or other sweetener
1/4 cup raw cashews soaked for 15 mins if needed, use 1/3 cup for creamier sauce, blended with 1/2 cup water until smooth
1/4 tsp cayenne to preference
cilantro for garnish

Directions

- Blend onion, garlic, ginger, chile with a few tbs. of water into a puree in a blender.
- Put Instant Pot on SAUTE. Add oil. When the oil is hot, add the onion puree. Cook for 3 mins, stir occasionally to avoid burning. (You can also saute without oil. Use broth and use finely chopped onion ginger garlic so that they dont stick)
- Meanwhile, blend tomatoes in the same blender until smooth and set aside.
- Add the spices and mix in. Add the pureed tomato and mix well to pick up and mix the sticking onion mixture so it doesnt burn while under pressure.
- Add the mushrooms and salt and mix well. (You can add other veggies or 1 cup cooked chickpeas/beans at this point). You dont need additional liquid as the mushrooms and veggies if using, will release moisture during cooking.
- Cancel SAUTE. Close the lid and PRESSURE COOK for 6 mins on HIGH PRESSURE. Once done, RELEASE THE PRESSURE after 10 mins.
- Add the peas, spinach, cashew cream, cayenne if using, and sweetener if using. Put the pot on saute and bring the mixture to boil.
- Taste and adjust salt, spice, flavor.
- Cancel SAUTE and serve garnished with lemon juice, cilantro.

Badam Halwa |Almond Pudding
Servings:4 Calories: 422 kcal Course: Dessert Prep Time: 5 mins Cook Time: 30 mins Total Time: 30 mins

Ingredients

1 tbs. ghee or unsalted butter
1 cup almond flour
5 tbs. slivered almonds
¾ cup almond milk

½ cup water
½ tsp. saffron
¾ cup sugar (adjust to taste)
½ tsp. cardamom powder

Directions

- Heat butter or ghee on Saute mode. Reserve 1 tbs. of slivered almonds for garnish and add the rest in. Add almond flour and saute for 3 to 4 mins.
- Add sugar to the almond mix and stir well.
- Heat milk, water and saffron in the microwave for 3 mins. Add the warmed saffron milk along with ground cardamom to the pot, and whisk well to prevent any lumps.
- Add saffron milk to the instant pot, Cancel SAUTE and close the lid. Set the vent to 'SEALING' mode and pressure cook for 4 mins on high pressure.
- After the cooking time, MANUALLY RELEASE THE PRESSURE and open the lid once the pin drops. Turn on SAUTE. Simmer the halwa to cook off the liquid. Stir at regular intervals to prevent burning.
- Cancel Saute when the halwa stops sticking to the pot and reaches a desired pudding like consistency. To check for doneness, take a tiny portion of the halwa in a spoon, cool for a minute, then gently roll it with your finger. If you're able to form a tiny ball, it's done. If it sticks to the spoon, simmer it for a few more mins.
- Do keep in mind that it continues to thicken as it cools. Garnish with the reserved slivered almonds and serve warm! Enjoy!

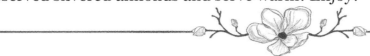

Whole Green Moong Dal

This is a simple high protein, delicious curry made with green lentils and spices.

Servings: 2 Calories: 156kcal Course: dal, Side Dish Prep Time: 6 hours Cook Time : 10 mins Total Time : 6 hours 10 mins

Ingredients

¾ cup dry Green gram/dry whole green mung lentil/moong dal
1 tsp. cumin seeds
1 large onion chopped
2 medium tomato chopped
1 tbs. ginger-garlic paste
3 green chillies split in half
1 tsp. salt adjust to taste

2-2.5 cups water
2 tablespoon coconut oil
cilantro/coriander leaves for garnish
juice of ½ lemon

Spices

¼ tsp. turmeric powder
½ tsp. cayenne or red chili powder (adjust to your preference)
1 tsp. coriander powder
1 tsp. garam masala/curry powder

Directions

- Wash and soak moong dal overnight (6-7 hours)
- Press SAUTE mode on Instant Pot. Add oil and once it's hot add cumin seeds. Let them crackle.
- Add ginger-garlic paste, saute till the ginger-garlic turns golden brown.
- Add onions, green chili and allow to saute for 2-3 mins until translucent -stir regularly
- Then add tomatoes and cook for 1-2 mins, till tomato turns soft.
- Add turmeric powder, red chili powder, coriander powder, garam masala and cook mixture for another 1 minute (avoid burning of spices)
- Now add soaked moong dal, water and salt give a stir. Close the lid on the pot and turn pressure valve from to SEALING position.
- Set the pot to manual (High Pressure) and set timer to 3 mins (for firmer moong beans) or 5 mins (for softer, broken up moong beans).
- Once the pot beeps, manually do a quick pressure release(QR).
- Remove lid away from you, add cilantro and lemon juice. Also adjust consistency of the dal at this point.
- Serve hot with any flatbread, boiled rice, roti, quinoa or eat as a soup

Chana Masala Biryani | Chickpeas Rice

Servings: 4 Calories: 458 kcal Course: Main Course Prep Time: 10 minsCook Time: 40 mins Total Time: 50 mins

Ingredients

Chana Masala

1 cup dried Chickpeas soaked overnight
1 tbs. ghee or olive oil
1 tsp. Cumin Seeds
1 tbs. ginger-garlic paste ½ inch ginger + 3 cloves garlic
1 medium onion sliced
2 green Serrano chillies or de-seeded Jalapeños for a milder flavor
1 large tomato chopped
1 tsp. salt
½ tsp. Turmeric Powder
1 tablespoon Garam Masala
1 tbs. Coriander Powder
2 tsp. Ground Cumin
½ tsp. Red Chili Powder or Cayenne Pepper
1 tsp. Smoked Paprika
1.25 cups water

Biryani

1 cup Basmati Rice Long grain (soaked and rinsed)
½ tsp. salt
½ cup Fried Onions
½ cup cilantro & mint, chopped
½ tsp. Saffron soaked in 1 tbs. warm-hot water.

Directions

- Prep: Rinse and soak basmati rice while you make chana masala. Slice onions and de-seed green chillies if you prefer mild heat. Chop tomatoes. Finely chop ginger garlic or pulse few times in a mini food processor.
- Making Chana Masala: Heat oil on SAUTE mode in Instant Pot. Add cumin seeds. When cumin seeds begin to sizzle, add onions and chillies and sauté for 30 seconds. Add ginger-garlic and sauté for another 30 seconds. Add chopped tomatoes and all spices listed under 'Chana Masala". Stir well and sauté for 30 seconds.
- Add rinsed and drained chickpeas and water. Stir well and close the lid. Set valve to SEALING mode. Cook on Bean/Chili mode or MANUAL for 25 mins.
- Biryani: After manual pressure release (QR), open the lid. Add drained rice. Sprinkle the remaining salt (listed under "Biryani"). Top with chopped cilantro & mint followed by soaked saffron (with liquid) and fried onions. Press down with a spatula gently. Close lid. Set valve to SEALING mode. Cook on MANUAL (high) for 6 mins.
- Open lid after NATURAL PRESSURE RELEASE. Using a fork, fluff the rice.
- Serve.

Aloo Matar| Peas Curry
This is a delicacy which is tasty and easy to make.

Servings: 4 Calories: 155kcal Course: Main Course, Side Dish Prep Time: 10 mins
Cook Time : 10 mins Total Time : 20 mins

Ingredients

4 medium regular potatoes OR 2 large Russet potatoes
1 cup green peas frozen, or fresh
1 tsp. cumin (jeera) seeds
1 medium onion finely chopped
1 tablespoon ginger garlic paste
1 green chilly finely chopped
1 cup tomato puree
2 tbs. cashew-nut cream OR fresh cream
2 tablespoon fresh cilantro/coriander leaves
2 tsp. lime juice or 1 tsp. amchur (dry mango) powder (optional)
salt as per taste
2 tbs. cooking oil
1 cup water

Dry Spices:

¼ tsp. turmeric powder
½ tsp. red chilli powder as required to your taste
1 tsp. coriander powder
1 tsp. garam masala powder

Directions

- Prepare tomato puree by adding 2 medium sized tomatoes into the blender with little water and keep aside.
- Press SAUTE mode on Instant Pot. Add oil in to the POT.
- Once oil is hot add cumin seeds, let the cumin splutter then add onions, ginger-garlic paste, green chili and fry until onions turn light brown.
- Next add prepared tomato puree, red chili powder, turmeric powder, coriander powder,garam masala powder and cook for 1-2 mins.
- Add peas, potatoes and salt and mix well.
- Then add water and give a stir.

- Close the lid on the pot, and turn pressure valve to SEALING position. Press CANCEL button on Instant Pot.Set the pot to MANUAL/PRESSURE COOK (High Pressure) and set timer to 3 mins.
- Once pot beeps, let the pressure release naturally for 5 mins and then Do a QUICK RELEASE.
- Remove lid away from you, add cashew-nut cream or fresh cream, lime juice and garnish with cilantro.
- Serve with hot with chapatis, roti & parathas.

Carrot Beans Poriyal Recipe

This is a very simple south indian stir fry recipe prepared with carrots, beans, fresh coconut with few spices in Indian style.

Servings: 4 Calories: 80kcal Course: Side Dish Prep Time : 10 mins Cook Time : 5 mins Total Time : 15 mins

Ingredients

1 cup carrot cut hbinto ½ inch pieces
1 cup green beans cut into ½ inch pieces
2 tsp. coconut oil
½ tsp. mustard seeds
½ tsp. urad dal
1 dry red chili
1 stalk curry leaves
2 green chili slit into half
a pinch asafetida(hing)
½ medium onion finely chopped
¼ tsp. turmeric powder
salt to taste
3 tbs. water
2 tablespoon fresh or frozen coconut shredded

Directions

- Wash and chop beans and carrots about ½ inch pieces.
- Press SAUTE mode on Instant Pot. Add oil in to the POT.Once hot, add mustard seeds, urad dal, dry red chilli, let mustard seeds splutter and dal turn light brown. Next add green chili, curry leaves and asafetida(hing). Saute for 15 secs
- Add chopped onion and saute till onions turn light brown in color.

- Next add green beans, carrots, turmeric powder, salt, water and mix well. Make sure to scrap of any spice if sticking to the pot.
- Close the lid on the pot, and turn pressure valve to SEALING position.
- Set the pot to MANUAL/PRESSURE COOK (High Pressure) and set timer to 1 MINUTE. When the instant pot beeps, Do a QUICK RELEASE.
- Remove lid away from you, add fresh shredded coconut and Mix well.
- Serve with hot rice, chapatis, roti & parathas.

Moong Dal Halwa|Indian Lentil Pudding

Servings: 4 Calories: 402 kcal Course: Dessert Prep Time: 5 mins Cook Time: 10 mins Total Time: 45 mins

Ingredients

½ cup Moong Dal (split mung beans)
1 cup water

After Pressure Cooking

½ cup Ghee
½ tsp Saffron soaked in ¼ cup hot milk
7 tbsp sugar, Adjust to taste while sautéing
½ tsp Ground Cardamom
2 tbsp chopped nuts (for garnish) (pistachios, almonds, cashews)

Directions

- Turn on Instant Pot on SAUTE mode. If your pot gets hot very quickly, switch to low (less) heat setting. Add moong dal to the pot.
- Dry roast the dal for about 10-12 mins until it changes from a pale yellow color to light golden. Stir at regular intervals during this time, especially the last 4 to 5 mins. It takes roughly 12 mins for this quantity. Cancel Saute and add water to the pot, and stir.
- If you use a separate sealing ring for desserts, switch to that. This step is optional.
- Close the lid and pressure cook for 10 mins at HIGH PRESSURE, on sealing mode.

- When cooking time is done, carefully RELEASE PRESSURE MANUALLY by pushing down the pressure valve (Ultra). If using a DUO model, turn the pressure knob to 'venting' position.
- Soak saffron in milk and microwave for 30 seconds while pressure is being released.
- Open the lid after the pin drops. Using a spatula, stir a few times to mash the cooked dal into a coarse paste.
- Select Saute mode (NORMAL). Add warmed melted ghee, saffron soaked in warm milk and sugar to the cooked dal. (Adjust the quantity of ghee to suit your preference).
- It is important to add warm milk and warm water. This prevents in any lump formations.
- Using a whisk or a spatula, stir everything together till combined well.
- Keep stirring at regular intervals to prevent the halwa from sticking to the bottom. Saute until it turns light golden brown in color, reaches a thick pudding-like consistency and ghee starts separating on the sides of the pot. Stir in ground cardamom. Remove the cooking pot from the base to prevent overcooking.
- Garnish halwa with chopped nuts like pistachio, almonds and cashews. Serve warm.

Masale Bhath

This vegetarian dish makes a great one pot meal and is made with a variety of vegetables and a warm spice blend.

Servings: 5 Calories: 430kcal Course: Entree, Lunch Prep Time: 20 mins Cook Time: 30 mins

Ingredients

1½ cups basmati rice
2 tbs. oil
⅛ tsp. hing {asafetida} optional
⅓ tsp. ground turmeric
1 medium onion sliced
1 tomato diced
1 to 2 green chilies minced
1 medium potato cubed
1 cup eggplant cubed
2 tsp. kosher salt
½ tsp. red chili powder

2 tsp. ginger grated
2 tsp. garlic minced
10 curry leaves chopped (optional)
¼ cup cilantro chopped
2½ cups water

Goda Masala Spice Blend

2 tsp.s coriander seeds
8 cloves
2 inch cinnamon stick
1 tsp. cumin seeds
1 tsp. brown sesame seeds
1 tsp. poppy seeds
1 tbs. unsweetened coconut shredded
2 green cardamom
15 black pepper

Garnish

½ cup cilantro chopped
2 tablespoon grated coconut (optional)
2 to 3 tbs. ghee (optional)

Directions

- In a small pan, roast all the spices for Goda masala on medium heat for about 2 to 3 mins until all the spices are hot to touch.
- Take the spices out in a bowl and allow them to cool. Once the spices are completely cool, grind them to a fine powder in a small spice jar. Reserve the Goda Masala spice blend.
- Set the Instant Pot to SAUTE mode and heat oil. Add hing and turmeric. Add onions and SAUTE for 2 mins. Add 1 tsp. salt, curry leaves, ginger, garlic and saute for a minute.
- Add tomatoes and mix well. Press cancel and saute for another minute, deglazing the bottom of the pot. Add potatoes, eggplant, remaining 1 tsp. salt, red chili powder, cilantro and mix well.
- Add the spice blend, rice, and water. Give a quick stir and close the Instant Pot lid with the pressure release valve to SEALING. Pressure cook on low pressure for 5 mins followed by 5-minute NATURAL PRESSURE RELEASE. Release the remaining pressure by turning the pressure release valve to venting.
- Open the Instant Pot and garnish with cilantro and coconut.
- Mix gently and top with ghee. Ghee can also be added while serving.

- Enjoy hot with yogurt or mattha.

Aloo Gobi

This is a healthy and delicious stir-fry made with potato, cauliflower that's infused with Indian spices.

Servings: 4 Calories: 175kcal Course: Main Course, Side Dish Prep Time: 10 mins Cook Time: 10 mins Total Time: 20 mins

Ingredients

1 medium Cauliflower head washed and cut into florets (about 3 cups)
2 small Potato cut into ½ inch cubes (about 1 cup)
1 tbs. Coconut oil
½ tsp. Cumin seeds(jeera)
1 tbs. Ginger Garlic minced
1 Green chili slit lengthwise
1 medium Onions finely chopped
2 small Tomatoes finely chopped (about 1 cup)
1 tbs. Lime juice OR 1 tsp. Amchur powder (Dry mango powder)
2 tbs. Cilantro/coriander leaves for garnish
4 tablespoon Water

Dry Spices

1 tsp. Red chilli powder
½ tsp. Turmeric powder
1 tsp. Coriander powder
1 tsp. Garam masala
Salt to taste

Directions

- Press SAUTE mode on Instant Pot. Add oil in to the POT.
- Once POT is hot add cumin seeds and let them splutter. Next add green chilli and minced ginger garlic and saute for 30 secs.
- Next add onions and saute until onions turn light brown.
- Add chopped tomatoes, then add in all the dry spices – coriander powder, turmeric powder, red chili powder, garam masala, salt.

- Then add potato cubes along with 2 tbs. of water and mix well. Cover the pot with a glass lid and let the potatoes cook for around 3-4 mins. You may stir them once in between.
- Remove the glass lid and add another 2 tbs. water to the pot and deglaze it. There shouldn't be any burnt bits at the bottom of the pot. Add the cauliflower florets and stir well.
- Press CANCEL button on Instant Pot.Close the lid on the pot, and turn valve from VENTING to SEALING position. Set the pot to MANUAL/PRESSURE COOK (Low Pressure) and set timer to 2 mins.
- Once the pot beeps, Do a QUICK RELEASE (QR)
- Remove lid away from you, add lime juice and garnish with cilantro. Mix well.
- Serve with hot with chapatis, roti, parathas or naan.

Gujarati Kadhi

Servings: 4 Calories: 159kcal Course: main course Prep time: 5 mins Cook time: 15 mins Total time: 20 mins

Ingredients

2 cups whole milk yogurt
¼ cup gram flour/chickpea flour (Besan)
2 cups water
2-3 tbs. powdered sugar
1-2 Thai green chilies finely cut
½ tsp. grated ginger
salt to taste
¼ cup finely chopped cilantro

For tempering

2 tsp. oil or ghee
½ tsp cumin seeds
½ tsp mustard seeds
A pinch asafoetida
1 sprig of curry leaves
2 chilies

Directions

- Add chickpea flour and yogurt to a saucepan. Whisk them together until completely mixed and no lumps remain.

- Add water, green chilies, sugar, and salt to the mixture and mix well. Set it aside.
- Set the Instant Pot on SAUTÉ Mode. Adjust the heat levels to 'Normal'.
- Pour oil or ghee into the steel pot. Once the display reads 'Hot', add cumin and mustard seeds.
- When the seeds crackle, add the asafoetida, curry leaves and chilies.
- Pour the chickpea flour -yogurt mixture into the steel pot and mix well.
- Press the Cancel button to reset the cooking program. Then select the Soup setting and set the cooking time for 6 mins.
- When the cooking program is complete, wait for 10 mins for the PRESSURE TO RELEASE NATURALLY. Move the pressure release valve to Venting to remove remaining pressure.
- Garnish with coriander and serve with rice or khichdi.

Gajar Halwa| Carrot Halwa
This tasty dessert is spiced with cardamom and served during festivals.

Servings: 4 Calories: 225kcal Course: Dessert Prep Time: 10 mins Cook Time: 25 mins Total Time: 35 mins

Ingredients

1 tbsp vegan butter or oil
3 tbsp cashews
3 tbsp chopped dates or raisins, or currants
2.5 cups of shredded carrots rainbow carrots
4 tbsp sugar
salt
1/4 cup almond meal
1/4 cup non dairy milk such as almond or soy
1/4 tsp ground cardamom
pistachios or cashews for garnish

Directions

- Put the Instant pot on SAUTE. Add vegan butter or oil.
- Add cashews and cook until golden. Stir occasionally. About 2-3 mins. Add dates/raisins and cook for a few seconds.
- Add carrots, sugar, salt and almond meal and mix well. Cook for a minute. Add non dairy milk and mix in.

- Close the lid. PRESSURE COOK for 6 to 7 mins MANUAL, HIGH in Instant pot. Let the PRESSURE RELEASE NATURALLY. Open the lid, Mix in the cardamom. Taste and adjust sweet if needed.
- Put the pot on SAUTE and cook the mixture for 3 to 4 mins to roast it well and to dry out the liquid. Stir well in between to avoid sticking.
- Add another 2 tsp vegan butter and mix in. Once the mixture starts to stick and is dry-ish. Switch off and let it sit.
- Let the carrot mixture SLOW COOK in the heat for 15 mins or so. Stir once in between.
- When the mixture is warm-cool, serve, or store refrigerated.
- Garnish with chopped cashews or pistachios to serve.

Palak Paneer Recipe
A one-pot Indian favorite with spinach and cottage cheese.

Servings: 4 Calories: 417kcal Course: Main Course Prep Time: 5 mins Cook Time: 15 mins Total Time: 20 mins

Ingredients

1 lb Spinach (Palak) washed
2 cups Paneer or Cottage cheese cut in bite sized cubes
1 tbsp Ghee or Oil
1 tsp Cumin seeds (Jeera)
1 Green Chili Pepper chopped
1 Onion medium, chopped
5 cloves Garlic chopped
1" inch Ginger chopped
1 Tomato medium, chopped
¼ cup Water
1 tsp Garam Masala

Spices

½ tsp Ground Turmeric
½ tsp Red Chili powder
1 tsp Coriander powder
1 tsp Salt adjust to taste

Directions

- Start the instant pot in SAUTÉ mode. Heat oil and add cumin seeds.
- When cumin seeds start to splutter, add ginger, garlic, green chili and onions. Sauté for 2 mins.
- Add tomato and spices. Stir and let it cook for 2 mins.
- Add water and deglaze the pot. Add in the spinach. Press cancel and close the instant pot lid with vent in sealing position. Set on MANUAL or pressure cook mode on HIGH PRESSURE for 2 mins.
- Once the instant pot beeps, do a 5 minute NATURAL PRESSURE RELEASE, which means release the pressure manually 5 mins after the beep.
- Blend the ingredients in the pot to a creamy texture using an immersion blender.
- Add the paneer and garam masala. Let it sit for 5 mins, so the paneer soaks in the flavors.
- Serve with naan, roti or paratha.

Mumbai Pav Bhaji

This is a popular Mumbai dish made up of spiced mashed vegetable curry, served piping hot with a soft bread roll with a butter, finely chopped onions, cilantro and a squeeze of lime.

Servings: 4 Calories: 267kcal Course: Breakfast, Main Course Prep Time: 10 mins
Cook Time: 20 mins Total Time : 30 mins

Ingredients

2 tbs. butter or oil
1 tablespoon ginger garlic paste
1 medium onion finely chopped
1 medium green OR red bell pepper chopped
4 medium tomatoes finely chopped (about 2 cups)
4 medium potatoes peeled and chopped (about 2 cups)
1 medium carrot diced
8 cauliflower florets (about 1 cup)
½ cup green peas
½ cup water
2 tablespoon pav bhaji masala available in Indian grocery store
1 tbs. kashmiri chilli powder
1 tbs. kasuri methi (dried fenugreek leaves) (optional)
salt to taste
1 tbs. lemon juice

For Pav:

12 pav or dinner rolls
¼ cup butter

For Garnish

¼ cup onion chopped
2-3 tbs. cilantro/coriander leaves to garnish

Directions

- Press SAUTE mode on Instant Pot. Heat 2 tablespoon of butter. Add in the ginger-garlic paste, onions and chopped capsicum/bell pepper. Saute until onions turn light brown.
- Next add in the finely chopped tomatoes. Mix well and cook for 1-2 mins till the tomatoes are soft.
- Add potatoes, carrots, cauliflower, green peas, salt and water.Mix well.
- Close the lid on the pot, and turn pressure valve from to SEALING position. Press CANCEL button on Instant Pot.
- Set the pot to "MANUAL/PRESSURE COOK" (High Pressure) and set timer to 6 mins. Once the pot beeps, wait for NATURAL PRESSURE RELEASE(NPR).
- Open and mash the Bhaji with potato masher or use immersion blender and coarsely grind the ingredients.
- Turn on the SAUTE again and add the red chilli powder, pav bhaji masala, kasuri methi (dried fenugreek leaves), lemon juice, salt and butter (optional but recommended). Let the bhaji boil for a 2 mins.
- Serve Bhaji with pav or bread rolls (Apply some butter and toast bread before serving).
- Garnish with butter, chopped onions and cilantro.

Easy Chana Dal | Split Chickpea Soup

Servings: 2 Calories: 106kcal Course: Soup Prep Time: 1 hr Cook Time: 45 mins Total Time: 1 hr 45 mins

Ingredients

For Dal:
1/2 cup split chickpeas (chana dal)
2 cups water

1 large tomato
3 cloves of garlic
1/2 inch ginger
1 tsp ground coriander
1/4 tsp turmeric
1/4 tsp paprika
1/4 to 1/2 tsp cayenne
1/3 to 1/2 tsp salt

For tempering:

1/2 tsp oil
1/2 tsp cumin seeds
a generous pinch of asafetida hing
1/2 tsp garam masala
1/4 tsp cayenne
1/4 cup chopped cilantro

Directions

- Soak the dal for 1 hour to overnight. Drain and combine with 2 cups water in a saucepan. Cover and cook for 20 to 25 mins over medium heat. Open the lid a crack if the water threatens to boil over.
- Meanwhile, blend the tomato, garlic, ginger, coriander, turmeric, paprika and cayenne with 1/2 cup of water until smooth.
- Add the tomato mixture and salt to the cooking split peas. Cover and cook for another 15 mins or until the split peas are tender. Mash some of the split peas and continue to simmer until desired tenderness and consistency.
- Make the tempering: Heat oil in a small skillet over medium heat. When the oil is hot, add cumin seeds and cook until they change color. half to 1 minute. Add in the asafetida. Add half of this tempering, garam masala, cayenne to the simmering dal and mix in.
- Taste and adjust salt and spice. Take off heat, add cilantro and mix in.
- Garnish with the remaining tempering and serve.

Printed in Great Britain
by Amazon